The New
RUSSIAN DIPLOMACY

The New
RUSSIAN DIPLOMACY

IGOR S. IVANOV

Foreword by Henry A. Kissinger

THE NIXON CENTER
and
BROOKINGS INSTITUTION PRESS
Washington, D.C.

Library of Congress Cataloging-in-Publication data

Ivanov, I. S. (Igor Sergeevich), 1945–
   [Novaëïa rossiæiskaëïa diplomatiëïa. English]
   The new Russian diplomacy / Igor S. Ivanov ;
foreword by Henry A. Kissinger.
       p.   cm.
Includes bibliographical references and index.
   ISBN 0-8157-4498-6 (alk. paper)
   1. Russia (Federation)—Foreign relations. I. Title.
   DK510.764 .I913 2002
   327.47—dc21   2002004633

9 8 7 6 5 4 3 2 1

The paper used in this publication meets minimum requirements of the American National Standard for Information Sciences—Permanence of Paper for Printed Library Materials: ANSI Z39.48-1992.

Typeset in Minion

Composition by Cynthia Stock
Silver Spring, Maryland

Printed by R. R. Donnelley and Sons
Harrisonburg, Virginia

CONTENTS

PREFACE

The Brookings Institution and The Nixon Center are pleased
to publish Russian Foreign Minister Igor S. Ivanov's book
The New Russian Diplomacy. During a period of new opti-
mism in the U.S.-Russian relationship, the Foreign Minister's
book can contribute importantly to American understanding
of the transformation of his country's foreign policy since the
collapse of the USSR.

Taking into account that Minister Ivanov is a sitting senior
official, his writing obviously reflects government positions.
Yet, his book presents Russian perspectives in a sophisticated
and eloquent manner. His description of the substance of
Russian foreign policy and its evolution contains much that is
not well known even among informed readers in the United
States. The book also includes the text of Russia's Foreign
Policy Concept, a Putin administration document that identi-
fies Russia's fundamental international interests and outlines
strategies to advance them.

The New Russian Diplomacy was originally published in
Russia, where it received largely favorable reviews. This volume
is a special edition prepared for American readers with a new

introduction and an expanded and updated discussion of the U.S.-Russian relationship. We are grateful to Carl Sandstrom for producing the English translation of the book and to Nikolas Gvosdev, executive editor of *The National Interest*, for his editorial assistance. We believe that the product is a useful and interesting contribution to the ongoing U.S.-Russian dialogue.

DIMITRI K. SIMES
President
The Nixon Center

MICHAEL H. ARMACOST
President
Brookings Institution

FOREWORD

In *The New Russian Diplomacy,* Foreign Minister Igor S. Ivanov provides a useful and intriguing assessment of the principal objectives of Russian foreign policy at the beginning of the twenty-first century. Unusually frank for a sitting government official, he also delivers a thoughtful analysis of the evolution of his country's relations with the United States and other key powers in the ten years since the collapse of the USSR.

Ivanov's discussion of the historical continuity in Russia's foreign policy—from the Russian Empire through the Soviet period to the present—is one of the most interesting aspects of the book, particularly to the American reader. Romantic enthusiasm for globalization and the Internet in the United States obscured the enduring nature of national interests in the post–cold war world. As a result, the inevitable disagreements of the 1990s, such as those over NATO's role in the Balkans, quickly produced frustration and disillusionment.

In this context, Ivanov's cool appraisal of Russia's current domestic and international challenges and his realistic definition of Russian interests—primarily oriented toward promoting the country's internal development while limiting losses to its international position—is noteworthy. Disagreements between Washington and Moscow will continue on issues like NATO enlargement and America's use of force abroad, but Ivanov's sober approach suggests that they can be managed. The two countries have a rare opportunity to work together in building a new international system.

HENRY A. KISSINGER
Honorary Chairman
The Nixon Center

The New
RUSSIAN DIPLOMACY

To the American Reader

This book is an attempt to analyze what has resulted from the foreign policy undertaken by the new Russian state over the last decade.

In 1991 Russia made a fundamental and historic choice in favor of democracy and a market economy. This decision had implications not only for domestic development, but for Russia's foreign policy as well. Radical transformation within Russia, in turn, helped to provide the impetus for a broad transformation of the entire global system.

For much of the twentieth century, Russian-American relations played a central role in international affairs. Even though relations between our two countries may not always have been the warmest, one thing was indisputable: this relationship decided the fundamental question facing the international community—whether there would be war or peace.

After the cold war ended, many began to doubt that the relationship between Russia and the United States would continue to be such a key element for world security. I believe that the tragic events that occurred in the fall of 2001 have dispelled any remaining doubts. The weeks and months following the September 11 terrorist attacks have convincingly demonstrated that the interaction of our two nations continues to be one of the primary driving forces in shaping world politics. Moreover, our relationship continues to be an important tool in responding to the new threats and challenges the world faces.

This is why the topic of Russian-U.S. relations constitutes such a large portion of this book. I felt it was important to show the evolution of relations between our countries the way it actually occurred, without embellishment and without simplification. It was obvious that after so many years of confrontation, our countries needed to overcome the dead weight of mutual distrust and outmoded political thinking and to change the very nature of our relationship. There have been uplifting moments of heightened expectations during this process, but also periods of serious disappointment.

And yet, I am convinced that over the past decade our two countries have managed to achieve what is most important: we no longer consider each other to be adversaries. Russian president Vladimir Putin emphasized this during his official visit to the United States in November 2001: Russian-U.S. relations should henceforth be based on common interests, shared values, and mutual respect. The unprecedented level of cooperation between Russia and the United States in the fight against international terrorism clearly confirms this. Our nations and peoples have demonstrated exceptional solidarity in the face of a common threat and have created a solid foundation for effective cooperation in dealing with future challenges to international peace and stability.

None of this means, of course, that every disagreement between Moscow and Washington has disappeared or that we will not disagree in the future. Yet it is important to recall the words of Thomas Jefferson: "Not every difference of opinion is a difference in principle." Today, we are united both by shared democratic values and by joint responsibility for maintaining world peace. As partners, we also share the responsibility of creating a new framework to ensure our strategic stability, by filling the legal void left in the wake of the U.S. decision to withdraw from the 1972 ABM Treaty. It is especially important to confer real legal authority to the agreements we have already reached on deep and verifiable reductions that are yet to come in the strategic offensive arsenals of Russia and the United States.

To put it simply, we still have a long and difficult way ahead. We are off to a good start, however, within the broad framework of the experience we have already achieved, working together on bilateral and international issues.

The Russian Federation desires to be a stable and predictable partner for its neighbors and friends around the world. Therefore, it is important to us that the deeper motivations of Russian foreign policy be correctly understood, by public opinion in Russia itself, as well as by our partners abroad. This is the main goal of this book—to help achieve such an understanding.

It is also the source of my desire to share with you, the American reader, my thoughts on what has been the outcome of the past ten years of Russian foreign policy.

So what are the results of the last decade?

I think we can state unequivocally that the Russian Federation today has come into its own as a democratic state with an independent and responsible foreign policy. Certainly, the main priniciples, priorities, and even the style of our foreign policy did not take shape immediately. Indeed, we had no real choice, for one of the world's two superpowers was now in the grip of a profound domestic transformation; and, seemingly overnight, we found ourselves in a completely changed geopolitical landscape, unable to find parallels anywhere in our thousand-year history to guide us.

Many in the United States surely remember how difficult and dramatic the rebirth of Russian democracy was, and, during the early and middle portions of the 1990s, how pointed and argumentative our discussions on foreign relations were. Today, we have a real opportunity to conduct a foreign policy that rests upon a general social and political consensus in Russia and is based on a clear vision of our national interests. Only with agreement at home on what constitutes the fundamental issues of our own national and social development can Russia navigate a sure and focused international course.

I have tried, here, not simply to describe the events of Russia's foreign policy, but also to show that there is, indeed, a certain logic guiding its development. This is why this book was conceived as a work of political analysis, and not as a memoir. The very nature of the questions posed requires such an approach. What stages has Russia gone through in laying the foundation of a new foreign policy? How has Russia resolved the key issues connected with the development of a complete presentation of its national interests and foreign policy priorities?

These questions cannot be answered without examining the historical roots of Russian foreign policy. At the beginning of the twentieth century, Sergei Sazonov (the last career diplomat to hold the position of minister of foreign affairs in the Russian Empire) wrote that ". . . all that is healthy and viable in political and civil life in any country must be carefully protected . . . and no reform called forth by current demands should be permitted to create a sudden break between the past and the present. Reform must be carried out gradually, so as to be made understandable by the people and not create the impression of a risk-filled experiment."[1]

At the end of that century—one filled with tragedy for Russia—we were forced to virtually redefine our role and our place in the world. Still, Russian diplomacy has never lost sight of the fact that its duty has been to represent the interests of a state that possesses a thousand-year history and a rich international tradition. Despite the radical change in Russia's geopolitics, it has only been possible to build an effective foreign policy by anchoring it on the firm foundation of historical continuity. And this, in turn, has required a reexamination of the legacy bequeathed by both the Imperial Russian and the Soviet schools of diplomatic thought.

I hope these digressions into the past will be of interest to the attentive American reader, particularly since they also touch upon the relationship between our two countries. Indeed, if one follows the trail of our two nations through history, it is striking to notice that despite their enormous differences, the destinies of both Russia and the United States have always crossed paths at key moments when beset by crisis or challenge. Moreover, they have almost always been willing to offer understanding and support to each other. This was especially true during the American War for Independence, as well as during the Civil War between the North and the South. Our nations were allies in the Second World War. In April 1943 Assistant Secretary of State Adolf A. Berle Jr. said, "The United States needs a strong, victorious Russia. . . . Over the last 150 years the presence of a strong Russia has been an important factor helping to guarantee America's security." This statement rings especially true today, when our nations are united by common democratic values.

Finally, I felt it was important to examine Russia's foreign policy with respect to the main trends in global development.

The world today is undergoing a transformation so deep and broad that it has no comparison in history. The international community has crossed the threshold into a new millennium on the wave of a veritable explosion that is transforming all facets of life and human endeavor. It is the dynamic nature of the changes taking place on our planet today that causes the complex and often dramatic collisions we see as we work to create a new system of international relations.

Although humanity is surely and confidently making progress in nearly all areas of science and technology, in the area of international relations we seem to be more akin to the ancient mariner sailing forth to discover new lands. The endless ocean stretches out before us, full of threats and dangers, with no sign of what land might appear on the horizon. The paradox of this scenario for our present situation lies in the fact that while the world has left behind the threat of global confrontation between the superpowers, it has been unable, so far, to make landfall on a new system of international security. The world community does not yet possess the tools it needs to counteract threats and challenges like those that manifested themselves so ruthlessly in the monstrous attacks on New York City and the Pentagon.

A fundamentally new approach to the development of foreign policy is needed. Discussion along these lines is being conducted in Russia as well as in the United States. Obviously, with the increasing interdependence of states, it is not enough simply to adapt one's foreign policy to a quickly changing world. It is essential to seek out ways to align one's national interests with the interests of the entire world community. In other words, not only should we be governed by democratic principles at home, we must also consistently observe them in our international relations. In my opinion, this is one of our primary obligations in this era of globalization.

As soon as the cold war ended, Russia found itself squarely at the center of the contemporary fundamental restructuring of international relations, as one of its primary catalysts. It is difficult to cite even one other historical example of a single country whose domestic social, economic, and political transformation had such deep and far-reaching consequences for the entire world community. Today, Russia conducts a foreign policy that seeks to reach its goals through partnerships with other states. At the core of this foreign policy lies a conviction that today's world faces global issues that equally affect the security and well-being of all nations. These issues can only, and must only, be addressed by working together.

I hope this book will help the American reader achieve a comprehensive understanding of the complex process by which a newly democratic Russia shapes its foreign policy, and that in so doing it will also make an important contribution to further understanding between our citizens.

1

AN OVERVIEW OF
RUSSIAN FOREIGN POLICY

Forging a New Foreign Policy Concept for Russia

Russia's entry into the new millennium was accompanied by qualitative changes in both domestic and foreign policy. After the stormy events of the early 1990s, the gradual process of consolidating society around a strengthened democratic government took hold as people began to recognize this as a requirement if the ongoing political and socioeconomic transformation of the country was to be successful. The formation of a new Duma after the December 1999 parliamentary elections, and Vladimir Putin's election as president of Russia in 2000, laid the groundwork for an extended period of political stability, which has allowed us to undertake the development of a long-term strategic development plan for the nation.

Russia's foreign policy course is an integral part of this strategic plan. President Putin himself has emphasized that "foreign policy is both an indicator and a determining factor for the condition of internal state affairs. Here we should have no illusions. The competence, skill, and effectiveness with which we use our diplomatic resources determines not only the prestige of our country in the eyes of the world, but also the political and economic situation inside Russia itself."[1]

Until recently, the view prevalent in our academic and mainstream press was that post-Soviet Russia had not yet fully charted its national course for development. It was often said that Russia needed a "new identity," that the country needed to establish a national "idea" or "mission." Without such a foundation, many found it impossible to conceive of an integrated, long-range foreign policy doctrine. The notion that our foreign policy is still "in the process of being formulated" consistently crops up in scholarly works published in recent years, both in Russia and abroad, and has even found its way into university textbooks describing contemporary international relations. However, there is now every reason to assert that the formative period of Russian foreign policy is essentially complete. The primary principles guiding the course of Russia's foreign policy, grounded in a clear understanding of the country's national interests, have been fully worked out.

Of course, no country's foreign policy begins with a blank slate. Despite the far-reaching transformation Russia experienced at the end of the twentieth century, the very fact that a state takes part in a global system of international relations presupposes the existence, for that state, of a defined set of underlying foreign policy goals that defines its place and its long-term interests in the international order. These conditions, of course, reflect the prevailing political forces at a particular instant in its history. They also, as a rule, spring from the objective characteristics of a country's particular historical, economic, cultural, and geopolitical development. These factors, in total, make up a kind of national foreign policy "constant," which is little affected by either domestic or international developments. In the history of diplomacy, the quality of continuity in foreign policy has been generally described by the saying "there are no permanent allies, only permanent interests." This continuity (even if it cannot be precisely measured) is characteristic not only of countries that are politically stable, but of all countries, including those, like Russia, that are in transition toward economic and sociopolitical modernization.

Contemporary Russia entered the global arena (following the breakup of the Soviet Union) possessing a tremendous amount of historical experience in international relations and a broad network of multilateral and bilateral relationships. Russia's foreign ties were based on the continuity provided by Imperial Russian and Soviet diplomacy. At the same time, however, it proved necessary to reformulate (and then to implement) positions taken by the government on a number of issues related to foreign policy, in order to reflect more adequately the characteristics of our nation's current stage of development and its position in the world.

On what basis, however, can we assert that today this process is largely completed? Above all else, the fact that a foreign policy doctrine, which Russian diplomacy was for so long accused of lacking, now exists—and it is not only on paper, but is actively guiding the day-to-day activities of the government. Russia's new Foreign Policy Concept, approved by the president on June 28, 2000, embodies this governing ideology (see appendix).[2] The Concept resulted from extensive analysis provided by politicians, civil servants, prominent social figures, diplomats, and academics of what the role and place of our nation in the world should be, especially at this particular point in the process of trying to realize our long-term national interests in the global arena.

That the new Foreign Policy Concept should appear at this time is no accident, of course. Its drafting was an integral part of the overall government strategy for national development and was closely wrapped up with the strategy's other components—the economy, state building, federal relations, social welfare, defense, and security. At the beginning of 2000, Russia adopted its National Security Concept, a primary document analyzing external threats to the interests of the Russian Federation.[3] Russia's Military Doctrine further develops the National Security Concept's positions on constructing defense. The Foreign Policy Concept does the same for specific areas of the government's foreign policy activity.

An important characteristic of the new Foreign Policy Concept is that it does not spell out rhetorical goals; instead, its aims are realistic and attainable. Nor does it completely reorient Russia's foreign policy course. The document primarily reflects tried and true principles and priorities that—and this is especially important—have been supported by the Federal Assembly and by popular opinion. In a word, this Concept is a working document, based on past experience and poised to go forward into the future. It provides Russian foreign policy with transparency and needed predictability. It gives the world community a clear road map to Russia's current actions and future steps in world affairs.

Defining this road map was no simple task. The effort was occasionally painful and was accomplished in several stages. In keeping with the adage that foreign policy is an extension of domestic policy, the process by which the new Russia became an entity in world politics reflected the depth and breadth of the internal changes our nation underwent in the final decade of the twentieth century.

The first of these stages was the period of Soviet *perestroika*, from 1985 to 1991. Two key events during this period helped shape Russia's new international role: the end of the cold war and the collapse of the Soviet Union. The second stage—from 1991 to approximately the mid-1990s—was the formative period in Russian foreign policy. This formative period proceeded concurrently with the establishment of a new socioeconomic order in Russia, attended by a full range of drastic, dramatic changes in the fabric of Russian life and in the very worldview of Russians. Not surprisingly, this formative period was distinguished by a fierce political struggle over the most basic issues of development, a struggle that directly affected our foreign policy.

In December 1991, Russia entered the global arena with a new appearance. Right from the start, Russia's foreign policy activity was carried out in a fundamentally new environment, one that differed from that of the Soviet period. This new legal and sociopolitical environment was characterized by

—radical change in the mechanism by which foreign policy was created; after the democratization of politics and society, the process was increasingly influenced by parliament, by the media, and by public opinion;

—less coordination in the development of international relations, which burgeoned as a result of Russia's increased openness to the outside world;

—swift and sometimes inappropriate moves by Russian regions and "subjects of the Federation"[4] to establish direct relations, bypassing the central government, with contiguous cross-border areas or with local authorities abroad;

—an abrupt transition to "openness" in information concerning foreign policy, coupled with the complete dismantling of the Soviet apparatus for engaging in foreign policy propaganda and the management of Russia's image abroad;

—the privatization of whole sectors concerning foreign relations that formerly were under strict governmental control, especially in relation to trade and economic cooperation, international investing, scientific and cultural exchanges, and so on.

This early formative period in Russia's foreign policy reflects the stormy and primordial process of establishing a democracy and market economy, with the attendant contradictions and costs.

The collapse of the Soviet political system occurred so suddenly and forcefully that at the time neither the leadership nor the Russian people had—and could not possibly have had—a full understanding of either what direction their country's development would take or what its foreign policy priorities would be. Russia's first president, Boris Yeltsin, addressed this directly and candidly in a 1992 speech before the Supreme Soviet:

> Russia's difficult transitional state does not allow us yet to discern its new or permanent character, nor does it allow us to obtain clear answers to the questions "What are we turning away from? What do we wish to save?" and "Which elements do we wish to resurrect and which do we wish to create anew?"[5]

The national consciousness was seized by the euphoria of change. To many it seemed that we had only to sharply alter our political orientation and the majority of our domestic and foreign affairs issues would resolve themselves. For example, our economic strategy was predicated on the belief that abrupt price liberalization and the institution of free market mechanisms would, by themselves, create a favorable dynamic for development. In foreign policy, we thus expected that a radical shift away from confrontation in favor of rapprochement with the West would automatically change the West's relationship to Russia and mobilize concentrated political support and economic aid for us. These unrealistic expectations clearly left their mark on the first draft of the Foreign Policy Concept, prepared in 1993.[6]

At the time, there really was substantial basis for such high hopes. The international climate had improved significantly during the late 1980s and early 1990s. The democratic changes in our country and the dramatic events of August 1991 in Moscow had evoked an enormous outpouring of sympathy for Russia and support of its leadership from across the globe. The majority of Russian popular opinion welcomed our rapprochement toward former adversaries and expected concrete returns for the country's new direction.

However, in actuality, everything turned out to be much more complicated. Ideological and domestic policy conflicts were exacerbated by seriously deteriorating socioeconomic conditions. Foreign policy was one of those areas where debates about which path Russia's development should take, and what Russia's relations with the West should be like, rose to the fore and were most pronounced. As in the nineteenth century, our relationship with the "West" (both as a defined bloc in international relations and as the embodiment of a particular model of socioeconomic and political development) had come to signify a particular ideological orientation.[7] On one side was displayed bellicose hostility toward Western civilization; on the other, an equally passionate desire to join the ranks of the West as quickly as possible, even if to the detriment of Russia's real interests.

In this regard, it is telling that Russia decided in the early 1990s to throw in its lot with accelerated integration into the Euro-Atlantic structure. Unrealistic goals were set forth; for example, to establish an "alliance" relationship with the West for which neither our country nor the West was prepared. Indeed, each side understood the concept in a completely different way. Many in the United States and Western Europe bought into the scenario that they had "beaten" Russia in the cold war and did not see a newly democratic Russia as an equal ally. At best, Russia was given the role of junior partner. Any manifestations of independence or attempts to defend its position were perceived as recidivism of Soviet "imperialist" politics. The move by the United States and NATO to expand the alliance right up to Russia's borders, in blatant disregard for Russia's national interests, was a clear wake-up call.

However, the period of an overt, idealistic pro-Western orientation in Russian foreign policy was relatively short-lived and superficial. Russian diplomacy quickly learned from it the appropriate lessons. This education was hastened by actual events: the creation of Russian foreign policy was being accomplished not in theoretical debates but "on the job," as

Russia strove to find solutions to real-life, complex international problems that bore directly on the country's national interests. After the collapse of the Societ Union it was necessary to "reorganize" the geopolitical space that remained and to create political mechanisms for regulating the conflicts that sprang up on the outer borders of the Commonwealth of Independent States (CIS). It was necessary to defend the rights of Russians who now found themselves outside Russia's borders, and to lay a new political foundation for relations with Central and Eastern European countries. In general, Russia had to fine-tune the ways in which it dealt with the entire rest of the world. These painstaking efforts—largely unseen by the public—are what dictated the logic of our foreign policy formation. These piecemeal efforts yielded the first conceptual conclusions that later were crystallized into established principles and a style for the Russian government's international activities.

These efforts did, however, have a significant result, in that Russia undertook its unprecedented, complicated, and painful internal transformation in a largely favorable and uncritical international environment. The Russian government had managed to avoid chaos along its borders with its new neighbors, to maintain national security at a level allowing for sharp cutbacks in military spending, and to mobilize broad international support for Russian reforms in both word and deed.

The very essence of the foreign policy problems faced by Russia disposed our country to evaluate international conditions realistically and take a pragmatic, rather than an ideological, approach to formulating aims and goals. The extremely contradictory international situation strengthened Russia's conviction that our only reliable foreign policy reference point was the consistent protection of our national interests. Only on this basis could we adequately respond to contemporary threats and challenges, consciously formulate positions on international issues, and forge purposeful relationships with other nations.

Foreign policy debates during in the 1990s often raised the (well-founded) question: what, specifically, were Russia's national interests? Indeed, Russia's specific course of action in the international arena directly depended on the answer to this question.

One legacy bequeathed by Soviet foreign policy was a "superpower mentality," which induced post-Soviet Russia to participate in any and all significant international developments, often incurring a greater

domestic cost than the country could bear. This approach was unacceptable, given Russia's enormous burden of unresolved domestic problems.
Common sense dictated that, for the time being, foreign policy should
first and foremost "serve" the vital interests of domestic development.
This meant providing reliable national security; creating the best possible conditions for sustained economic growth; increasing the standard of
living; strengthening the country's unity, integrity, and constitutional
order; and defending the rights of citizens and compatriots abroad.

From all of this, another conclusion was reached: the need for an "eco-
nomical" and focused approach, rejecting gratuitous or superfluous
diplomatic efforts in favor of an active, multivectored foreign policy that
took advantage of anything that might produce real returns for domestic development. Yevgeny Primakov, Russia's minister of foreign affairs
from 1996 to 1998, remarked,

> . . . in the absence of any active foreign policy, it is difficult if not
> impossible for Russia to effect any fundamental domestic transfor-
> mations or preserve its territorial integrity. Russia is far from indif-
> ferent about the manner and capacity in which she enters the world
> economy: as a mistreated appendage useful as a source of raw
> materials, or as an equal participant. In many ways, this also relates
> to the function of foreign policy.[8]

In other words, the need to focus on solving domestic problems in the
context of foreign policy in no way signifies xenophobia or a retreat into
isolationism. On the contrary, rational diplomacy on issues of vital
importance to Russia and the world community can, in some cases, make
up for a lack of economic, military, and other domestic resources.

Concrete foreign policy experience has also brought clarity to the
issue of what was the best line to take in relations with the leading countries of the West. Today, not only among politicians and diplomats but in
Russian society in general, there is a clear understanding that unjustified
concessions to the detriment of our national interests, on one hand, and
slipping into confrontation with the United States, Europe, and Japan, on
the other, are both unacceptable extremes. Foreign policy aimed at consistent and, where necessary, strict defense of national interests in no way
contradicts the goal of increasing Russia's participation both in the com-

munity of democratic nations and in the global economy. In particular, this has been borne out by the experience of Russia's consistent efforts to integrate into the activities of the G-8. Within this authoritative forum, Russia actively participated in discussions with the leading industrially developed powers on issues of key importance for both regional and global security and stability. No matter how complicated the problems that Russia faces in its relationship with the more developed countries, Russian diplomacy should strive for constructive cooperation and joint exploration of mutually satisfactory solutions. It is in Russia's interests to widen its circle of friends and partners in the world, as this can only strengthen the Russian state.

Notably, this approach is endorsed by Russian academic experts. A report prepared by the Russian Independent Institute of Social and Nationalities Problems emphasizes that Russian foreign policy

> has become more balanced toward the West and the East; foreign policy began to correspond more with the country's national interests. Russian experts do not agree with the point of view, especially prevalent among a segment of Western analysts, which states that Russian foreign policy is increasingly confrontational toward the West. The majority of them believe that Russia's foreign policy course, despite the changes it has undergone, remains appropriately balanced and is not excessively strict toward the West.[9]

Posing the problem in this way is the key to understanding another eternal question, being asked more and more often: is Russia a Western or an Eastern power? Experience has demonstrated the futility of trying to juxtapose different supposed geographical delineations of Russian foreign policy. The unique geopolitical position of our country—not to mention the realities of world politics and economics—dictate the necessity for Russia to cultivate cooperation equally with nations to our West, East, North, and South. This was well understood by prominent Russian thinkers of the past. Developing a long-range concept for Russia's industrial development at the end of the nineteenth century, the great Russian scientist Dmitri Mendeleev (1834–1907) stated that national interests demanded the development of trade and economic relations with neighbors to the West and the East. He had no doubt that "all Russia's politics would sooner or later be guided by this circumstance."[10] Indeed, many of our historians have asserted that in the cultural scheme of things, Russia functions as a bridge between the two great Western and Asian civilizations. Having incorporated the traditions and values of East and West, Asia and Europe, Russian civilization is a unique phenomenon.[11]

Thus, over time, fundamental principles were established, and these have become the basis for the updated Foreign Policy Concept. Its contents were stipulated not only by the country's domestic goals and interests, but also by the need to determine Russia's position in the face of new global challenges and to decide what system of international relations best meets the country's interests.

In the Concept, the problem of how economics and foreign policy are interrelated is addressed anew. In the transition to a market economy, priority has been given to goals including strengthening the Russian economy and rebuilding those specialized areas geared to the international economy; facilitating full membership and participation in international economic organizations; helping Russian entrepreneurs enter foreign markets; attracting foreign investment; and solving the issue of our foreign debt. Russian diplomacy has become actively engaged in seeking ways to minimize the negative effects of globalization on our country and to create in Russia the conditions necessary for sustained economic growth and economic security.

The most important principle of the new Foreign Policy Concept is that one of the primary measures of the effectiveness of Russian foreign policy will be the degree to which the rights and interests of Russian citizens—no matter where they are or where they live—are protected. The significance of the "human dimension" in Russian diplomacy has sharply increased. First and foremost, this means ensuring the rights of millions of Russian citizens living outside Russia in countries belonging to the former Soviet Union.[12]

Also of critical significance has been the complete overhaul of the process by which foreign policy is crafted. The democratization of society, coupled with the creation of a law-based government, has had a significant impact on the way policy is determined. Specifically, it was necessary to delineate what role would be played by the parliament in making foreign policy decisions, to spell out the interrelationship of the legislative and executive branches, and to apportion authority between the president, government, and regional authorities for conducting foreign affairs. Thus, domestic political reform has had a considerable effect on our approach to foreign policy issues.

It was also necessary to revisit the way information about foreign policy is conveyed to the public. Over the past ten years, the mass media's influence on the formation of public opinion has grown rapidly, with extremely varied consequences. Thus, the Russian foreign policy establishment has found it necessary to develop a new style and new ways of interacting with the media. It has had to learn to work in an environment characterized both by transparency and by pluralism.

Finally, the new reality apparent in Russia, as well as changing world conditions, have made renovation of the diplomatic service unavoidable. In this regard, a key goal will be to ensure stability and continuity from one generation of Russian diplomats to the next by adequately training and preparing new diplomatic cadres to meet the international relations demands of today and the future.

The enormity of these issues illustrates the number and complexity of the stages through which Russian foreign policy has had to go in the last decade of the twentieth century.

Continuity in Russian Foreign Policy

Continuity is a critical component in any state's foreign policy and diplomacy. It has both great theoretical and great practical importance. It is difficult to imagine any serious evaluation of the state's role and place in international affairs—or evaluation of its political culture and style, and methods of diplomatic practice—without taking into account elements of continuity.

Continuity is generally understood as "a connection between phenomena in the developmental process in nature, society, and cognition whereby the new replaces the old but preserves some of its elements." In society, continuity denotes the transfer and incorporation of social and cultural values from one generation to the next, achieved in its totality by following traditions.[13] With regard to foreign policy and diplomacy, continuity can be defined as the sum of those internal and external factors that (1) have long-lasting effects on the formation of foreign policy and on the style and methods of a given state's diplomacy, and (2) retain in some form or other their significance in a constantly shifting domestic and international landscape.

It is natural that continuity in foreign policy becomes a hot topic during periods of revolutionary change and radical reform. Elements of continuity often run counter to the new features that arise in foreign policy after abrupt sociopolitical shifts. In reality, however, this juxtaposition is completely conditional. No state can recreate its foreign policy from scratch simply because of particular domestic political changes, even if such change is profound. Foreign policy objectively reflects the characteristics of how a country—its culture, economy, geopolitical situation—have historically developed, and therefore is a complex alloy, comprising elements of both continuity and renewal, which defies expression in an exact formula. It is common that what appears to be a fundamentally new direction for foreign policy actually turns out to be yet another variation of a traditional policy repackaged in a form more in line with the spirit of the times.

In practice, continuity of foreign policy is an important factor in the stability of international relations. In a narrow sense, continuity is defined as the degree to which a state remains true to its international obligations. In a wider sense, it indicates a state's ability to act as a predictable and responsible member of the world community. Also, in a democracy, foreign policy continuity presupposes sufficiently broad public agreement inside the country as to the basic course and direction of policy. In and of itself, this consensus is a measure of a certain level of development and maturity of a state's political system.

Issues of continuity for foreign policy and diplomacy are especially critical for Russia, which for centuries has played an important role in European and world affairs. Twice during the twentieth century, Russia underwent profound internal transformations that, in turn, had profound effects upon its foreign policy.

According to a recently published work on the history of nineteenth-century Russian foreign policy, the modern methodology for studying foreign policy takes a complex approach encompassing a wide range of events and phenomena. This is because a country's foreign policy and state mechanism function within the framework of two socioeconomic and political systems: intrastate, where foreign policy originates, and interstate, where it is carried out. Therefore, foreign policy analysis must take into account the political and socioeconomic aspects of national policy, the sociopolitical system of a country as well as its geography and demography, its industrial and military resources, cultural level, national consciousness, the political mentality of the ruling circles and of the populace, the particulars of its history, its traditional relationships with the rest of the world, and so on and so forth.[14]

It is easy to see that most of the factors cited above as influencing a state's foreign policy are long term and often continue to operate even through periods of far-reaching national and international change. Taken together, these factors also determine the continuity of a state's foreign policy and diplomacy.

Twentieth-century Russian history yields many examples of how, during periods of radical revolutionary change and during the most profound internal sociopolitical transformation, foreign policy and diplomacy have continued to embody the nation's basic goals and national interests. It is telling that despite an apparently complete ideological split with the diplomatic traditions of the Russian Empire, Soviet approaches did not negate this continuity. In particular, noted Soviet historian and foreign policy expert Boris Shtein wrote (in a foreword to the memoirs of tsarist diplomat Yu. Ya. Solov'ev) that "not everything about Russian diplomacy from the end of the nineteenth to the beginning of the twentieth centuries should be crossed out. Many of the goals and objectives sought by Russian diplomacy retained their significance despite the overthrow of the tsarist regime. These goals belonged not to tsarist Russia, but to Russia as a nation and to the Russian people."[15]

Of course, Western analysts saw Soviet foreign policy, especially during its final decades, as historically continuous. George Kennan, one of the founders of American Sovietology, wrote that "the history of Russian statesmanship and diplomacy, including that of the Soviet period, has been marked by some rather striking elements of continuity."[16] Kennan attributed the foreign policy peculiarities of the Soviet period to an "ideological superstructure" that was "superimposed" in 1917 onto the essentially unchanged foreign policy legacy of previous eras.[17] Like many other American historians, Kennan identified this legacy with negative traits of Russian "imperial" policy, such as a tendency toward territorial expansion, claims of "ideological exclusivity," deep mistrust toward the West and foreigners in general, and so forth. Thus, American Sovietologists see continuity in a negative light.

Undoubtedly, assessments like these are one source of the stereotypes about Russia and its foreign policy that are deeply embedded in the Western psyche. These stereotypes continue today to help perpetuate mistrust and even hostility toward modern Russia in certain circles in the West, especially in the United States.

This underscores the critical need to understand the experience of Russian foreign policy and diplomacy in their modern context. It is even more important because the processes of establishing a new Russian state and building a new national consciousness make active reference to Russian history and tradition. Russian society looks to its own history to provide the vital reference points it needs to fill the political and psychological vacuum left by the fall of the old system. This is where Russia looks to form a new value system—a system that must be founded on firm historical ground to remain stable. To paraphrase Alexander Herzen (1812–70), Russian society is "sizing up the modern day by more fully understanding the past; discovering the meaning of the future by more deeply delving into what has passed; and striding ahead by looking back."

What is the overall conceptual framework for understanding continuity in modern Russian foreign policy with regard to the Soviet and pre-Soviet periods? In what areas of history is full knowledge and understanding most useful to ensure Russia's foreign policy interests and improve its diplomatic service today?

The complexity of the answers to these questions lies in the fact that current Russian foreign policy cannot be described either as a direct continuation of Soviet foreign policy or as an automatic restoration of the foreign policy pursued by the tsars and the Provisional Government that was interrupted in 1917. This is because the "Russian Federation" that entered the global arena in December 1991 was a state qualitatively different from all of its predecessors. Its modern political system had no analogue in Russian history, and both its territorial configuration and its immediate geopolitical environment were markedly different. In these respects, Russia was a completely new state and therefore needed to develop a new way of looking at its foreign policy goals and priorities. It needed to take into account changed domestic and international realities. Forging a new approach, however, could not be accomplished overnight. The new state needed time to develop and inculcate a new set of foreign policy priorities in the national, political, and popular consciousness.

Although in some respects a "new" state, the Russian Federation that emerged after the collapse of the Soviet Union also came equipped with centuries of international experience, it had an existing infrastructure for bilateral and multilateral relations, and was the heir to a rich legacy provided by the professional Russian and Soviet schools of diplomacy. However, inheriting and assimilating this experience was not, and could not have been, automatic. The formation of a new Russian foreign policy was a creative process right from the start. Objectively, the process became a complex synthesis of the Soviet legacy, resurrected Imperial Russian diplomatic traditions, and completely new approaches dictated by the fundamental changes that had occurred in Russia and the world.

Because the Soviet Union had not made its exit into history as the result of a military defeat or violent social revolution, Russian foreign policy was intertwined with both wholly new elements and elements continuous with the past. Russia had broken with Soviet ideology yet purposefully retained all that was positive in Soviet foreign policy and that continued to meet Russian national interests. Unlike the Revolution of 1917, which severed centuries of foreign policy tradition and physically liquidated Imperial Russia's diplomatic service, the new democratic state preserved intact much of the Soviet apparatus, both in terms of agencies and of personnel.

This approach was in complete accordance with the stance adopted in 1991, which conceived of the Russian Federation as the continuation of and rightful successor to the USSR. It is telling that Russian diplomacy's first practical efforts were aimed at ensuring that this concept gained international acceptance. The first step in this direction was the December 24, 1991, message from the president of the Russian Federation to the secretary-general of the UN regarding the continuation of the Soviet Union's UN membership by the Russian Federation. The message also requested that responsibility for all the USSR's rights and obligations according to the UN Charter be transferred to the Russian Federation.[18] A note from the Russian Foreign Ministry dated January 13, 1992, states that the Russian Federation "continues to ensure the rights and fulfill the obligations of international agreements signed by the USSR."[19] International acceptance of this was of enormous practical importance to Russia at that particular time, in that it gave Russia a permanent seat in the UN Security Council and helped solve many complicated issues of rightful succession with regard to relations with former Soviet republics.

Nevertheless, the new Russia could not see itself as heir to the USSR in the aspects of a foreign policy that had been dictated by "class struggle" on the international arena and that had led to conflict with the United States and other Western countries. Not only had this opposition resulted in the flare-up of acute international crises like the 1962 Cuban missile crisis, which led the world to the brink of nuclear war; it had also fueled the arms race and drained the Soviet economy. In the end, this was also one of the primary reasons for the collapse of the Soviet Union and the socialist bloc.

It would, however, be a mistake to say that the foreign policy experience of the Soviet period was driven solely by confrontational ideology. Being the incarnation of the Russian state at the time, the Soviet Union built its foreign policy in terms of the way it understood its national interests. This was demonstrated by Soviet diplomatic efforts aimed at averting the threat of global nuclear conflict, regulating international crises, and facilitating peaceful coexistence and cooperation between countries with opposing sociopolitical systems. Historic achievements in this vein included the creation of the United Nations, the signing of the Helsinki Accord, and the development of a complex system of Soviet-American and international treaties and agreements on arms control and disarmament.

Indeed, some of the most enduring legacies in the international system today were forged during the Second World War. As a result, the experience of the international role played by the Soviet Union during this period holds lasting significance, even for Russia's foreign policy today. The foundations of the postwar order first took shape during the wartime meetings of the heads of state of the anti-Hitler coalition. Conceptually, this new world order was designed not only to ensure global peace and international security, but also to facilitate continued cooperation between the member-states of the wartime alliance. Working together, the allies struck a compromise on the disposition of postwar Germany. Democratic resolutions were found for settlement with former German allies, with whom peaceful treaties were signed (with the exception of the treaty between the USSR and Japan).

A special place in the postwar world order belonged to the formation of the United Nations. Before the eyes of the United Nations' founding fathers was the lamentable experience of the League of Nations, created after World War I. The League of Nations was unable to ward off the aggressive acts of Germany, Italy, and Japan during the 1930s and unable to halt the unfolding of World War II. The League of Nations was unable to solve disarmament issues. However, it was during the 1930s that the idea of collective security was developed. Although never put into practice, as a concept, collective security was aimed at strengthening peace and stability and greatly influenced the development of international relations. The experience of trying to achieve collective security in Europe was put to active use by the Allied powers in their fight against fascism.

Soviet diplomacy not only helped make victory over the Axis powers possible, but also made an important contribution to postwar efforts to draft permanent and final settlements in Europe and the world. Soviet diplomacy also figured significantly in the formation of the United Nations, whose charter essentially became the primary legal basis for modern international relations. A key principle of the UN is that it has, from the start, been oriented toward the future. The ideas and principles contained in the UN Charter bear witness to the far-reaching vision of the organization's founders, who created it as a universal body to serve as the backbone for international relations. Today, amidst globalization and the gradual trend toward a more multipolar world system, it is difficult to find an organization that better meets the demands of the times. It is no accident that those who seek to impose a "one-size-fits-all" model of world order focus their primary efforts on weakening the UN's role and excluding it from the process of solving today's critical issues.

History has carried out a just verdict against the cold war and its extremely negative effect on international relations in the postwar period. More than once during these years did the threat of nuclear disaster hang over the world. At the same time, even at the most dramatic and difficult periods, the great powers—primarily the USSR and the United States—successfully managed to reach mutually acceptable compromises in order to avoid a fatal confrontation. Numerous local crises notwithstanding, the cold war did not escalate into a "hot" global conflict. This outcome was helped not only by the will and wisdom of individual world leaders of the time, but also by the specific mechanisms that existed to support international stability and that were inherent to the bipolar world order of the postwar decades.

It was also during the cold war that the prerequisites for a multipolar system of international relations were put into place. Despite the obvious preeminence of the USSR and the United States, other influential factors also coalesced and had an effect. One such factor was the Non-Aligned Movement. The fall of colonialism drew into the sphere of active international politics dozens of African and Asian countries, which gradually cultivated their input into growing international cooperation. They advanced many initiatives that, in large measure, facilitated the democratization of international relations. The inclusion of Asian, African, and Latin American countries as equal members in the political big leagues was one of the most remarkable developments of the postwar world. In its relations with these countries, Russia today relies in large measure on the goodwill and mutual sympathy created during the years in which the USSR supported their quests for political independence and economic self-sufficiency. Russian diplomacy actively uses this reservoir of goodwill in the interests of ensuring global security and the stability of democratic development throughout the world.

The most important outcome of the postwar period was the creation of a complex system of international treaties and agreements on disarmament. This is when the key Soviet-American agreements were signed that laid the foundation for strategic stability and for the subsequent limitation and reduction of nuclear weapons and other weapons of mass destruction. To this day, these agreements remain an indispensable aspect of international security. Against the background of today's intense struggle to determine the fundamental basis of the future world order, the merits of the development and promotion by Soviet diplomacy of numerous major multilateral agreements and treaties on arms control clearly stands out. Among these, the Non-Proliferation Treaty and the Convention on Chemical Weapons will undoubtedly retain their enduring significance for ensuring peace.

Although the bipolar world in which all these agreements and treaties were negotiated and signed has gone forever, the world community has yet to create any new, more effective means of ensuring world peace and stability. It is no accident, therefore, that the fight to preserve the 1972 ABM Treaty grew into such a major issue in international politics.

The postwar experience retains its full relevance for current issues of European security. It was in Europe during the late 1960s and early 1970s that it yielded positive developments like the relaxation of international tension and the related pan-European process that produced the Helsinki Final Act. The experience in compromise during the negotiations on European détente is clearly not only of historical significance; it also serves the goals and objectives of today. It also brilliantly illustrates how effective solutions are possible only by addressing mutual interests and seeking mutually acceptable compromise.

The issue of human rights was central from the 1960s through the 1980s. During this period, the Soviet Union joined the European process to gradually become more involved in the issue and was a signatory to international understandings on various human rights questions. The fact that Soviet foreign policy and diplomacy had addressed human rights certainly helped during the subsequent radical democratic reforms in Russia.

Despite this important legacy, the simplified nihilistic view of Soviet foreign policy and diplomacy is foreign to today's Russian diplomacy. Recent evaluation of Soviet foreign policy has begun to take an increasingly cold and scientific approach, based on painstaking analysis of both positive and negative experience, carefully sifting through this legacy in order to preserve the best traditions of national diplomacy. One of the most striking examples of this approach was a 1999 Moscow academic conference coinciding with the ninetieth anniversary of former Soviet foreign minister Andrei Gromyko's birth.[20]

Such is not the case with the assimilation of the Russian foreign policy and diplomacy legacy from the period before 1917. Here, the challenge was to resurrect and interpret the significance of individuals and events that were either relegated to oblivion or undeservedly slandered or discredited during the Soviet period. The numerous scientific conferences, discussions, and publications devoted to such topics as the 450th anniversary of the *Posolsky Prikaz* (the Muscovite Foreign Office), the 200th anniversary of the birth of Prince Aleksandr Gorchakov (1798–1883), and the life and work of great Russian diplomats and scholars like Fyodor Fyodorovich Martens (1845–1909) and Pavel Nikolayevich Miliukov (1859–1943) have been important in this regard. Today, plans are under way for an entire schedule of events and activities dedicated to the 200th anniversary of the founding of the Russian Foreign Ministry, which will be commemorated in 2002.

A particular role in developing the Foreign Policy Concept, for example, was played by the discussions surrounding the jubilee celebrations for Aleksandr Gorchakov. Gorchakov is inseparably linked with the most brilliant pages in the history of Russian diplomacy. He directed Russian diplomacy during a period of broad liberating reforms in the second half of the nineteenth century.[21] These reforms began after Russia had been weakened by the Crimean War and was in danger of becoming a second-rate state, relegated to the background of the "Concert" of Europe. In a memorable note to Emperor Alexander II, Gorchakov characterized the task of foreign policy in this way:

> Our policies should pursue a double goal. First, to keep Russia safe from becoming involved in any kind of external complications that could divert some of our effort away from our own internal development. Second, we must make every effort during this time to ensure that no changes—either territorial or in the balance of power and influence—occur in Europe that might seriously dam-

age our interests or political situation. . . . If we attain these two goals, we can hope that Russia will recover from its losses, become stronger, and replenish its resources, to regain its position, authority, influence, and destiny among the great powers. . . . Russia will be able to attain this only by developing its internal strengths, which in this day and age are the only true sources of a state's political might.[22]

Despite all the differences between Russia's circumstances in the middle of the nineteenth century and those of today, our country faces two complex foreign policy challenges that were familiar to Gorchakov: creating the most favorable conditions possible for internal reform while—and this is the other side of the same coin—not allowing the country's international position to be weakened.

A significant social and cultural event for Russia, the Gorchakov jubilee made it possible not only to pay deserved tribute to a great Russian civil servant and diplomat, but also to assimilate into practice his legacy, which resonates surprisingly well with the foreign policy challenges faced by Russia today. Gorchakov's basic principles—pragmatic evaluation of international processes, using national interests as a foundation, and the defense of national interests even in the most difficult conditions—are of enduring significance for Russia today, in a completely different historical era. Therefore, it is logical that the outcome of the events commemorating Gorchakov has become an integral part of the new world vision and role that Russia is developing in world affairs.

Comprehensive analysis of Gorchakov's legacy played a certain role in the development of the reworked Foreign Policy Concept of the Russian Federation. The essence of the new Concept has something in common with these words of Gorchakov:

. . . No matter in what area—Europe or the East—we seek to make suppositions, we reach the same conclusion: for our own security and for the sake of our might abroad . . . in the interests of peace and overall balance, Russia's first and foremost duty is to its own successful transformation, on which the future of Russia and all Slavic peoples depends. This is the fundamental basis of our policy.[23]

This approach to our primary foreign policy goals is a long-standing tradition in Russian diplomacy. Russian diplomacy's potential has been most often called upon in times of difficulty, such as at the beginning of the seventeenth century, the "Time of Troubles," when political uncertainty and foreign intervention significantly weakened Russia's international status.[24] Nevertheless, Russia quickly regained its international authority, participating as a guarantor of the 1648 Peace of Westphalia, which established general principles of international relations that have lasted for centuries, most notably the concept of state sovereignty.

Later—especially during the periods of serious crisis following our 1905 defeat by Japan in the Russo-Japanese War and after the first Russian Revolution of 1905–07—Russian foreign minister Aleksandr Izvolsky (1856–1919) and his successor, Sergei Sazonov (1861–1927), considered it their main goal to ensure the lasting peace and stability needed to carry out the reforms proposed by Prime Minister Petr Stolypin.[25] Sazonov wrote:

Russia, shaken by disaster in the Far East and by the outbreak of a revolution at home that was difficult to put down, urgently needed peace making and careful legislative work—the only thing that would lead the nation toward the political and economic reform that had been poised to take root.[26]

There is a certain logic in the fact that during periods such as these, Russian diplomacy not only facilitated the creation of foreign conditions favorable for the reform of government and society; it also, on an intragovernmental level, tended to work in favor of patriotic, liberal, and moderate reformist forces. In particular, Aleksandr Gorchakov played a prominent role in effecting a gradual transition away from the old feudal understanding of diplomacy as a personal service to an autocratic monarch and toward the concept of diplomacy for the purpose of attaining national interests. Gorchakov, in his dispatches, was the first to use the phrase "the Sovereign and Russia." "Before me," he wrote, "Europe had for us only the concept of 'Emperor.' Count Nesselrode once even reproached me for using the expression. 'We only know the Tsar,' said my predecessor. 'We have nothing to do with Russia.'"[27]

Gorchakov also proudly reminisced about his role in Alexander II's decision to rehabilitate the surviving Decembrists,[28] restore their ranks and titles, and allow them to return from exile.[29] He is also known for supporting other liberal initiatives during reform periods in the second half of the nineteenth century.

During the Stolypin reforms, members of the Russian foreign policy establishment were among the most consistent supporters of progressive constitutional transformation. One of them in particular, Izvolsky, has been described by modern historians as

a new breed of statesman for a modern era. He was a dynamic and pragmatic politician of broad, yet quite moderate, political views. Gorchakov was not locked into the framework of international politics. He established a working partnership with legislative bodies, with the press, and with representatives from political parties, finance, and industry to bring tsarism out of its deep domestic and foreign policy crisis, to broaden the class basis of its foreign policy, and to strengthen Russia's standing as an international power.[30]

S. D. Sazonov continued this approach to domestic policy. When making reports to Nicholas II, Sazonov wrote in his memoirs that "in discussing foreign policy issues, I would constantly come up against Russia's domestic situation, which was becoming increasingly volatile under the influence of revolutionary propaganda."[31] According to his colleagues, Sazonov frequently held a decisive position in counterbalance to those within the regime who leaned toward all manner of retrograde and Black Hundred elements.[32]

"Enlightened patriotism" has characterized the political culture of Russian diplomacy throughout history. The Russian diplomatic service has always taken an impartial, professional, and realistic approach to any evaluation of the domestic situation, tending to view domestic events in relation to Russia's national interests. Russian diplomacy has thus been free of any kind of extremism or adventurism, and has been based in common sense and a desire for what is best for Russia.

It would appear that the task of modern Russian diplomacy, and of all those involved in Russia's international activities, is to gradually overcome the great shift in psychology and values that came after 1917. Serious analysis and assimilation of our diplomatic history will allow us to regain continuity in our national development and in our foreign policy. Our solution to this problem will essentially form the "national idea" that is so badly needed by the politically aware and nationally involved portion of Russian society and that would serve as a stable basis for national consensus on fundamental foreign policy issues.

In particular, it is important to restore continuity in the accurate social perception of the active foreign policy that Russia traditionally had and which for centuries not only ensured that our country played a leadership role in world politics, but also guaranteed our national security. At all stages in history, indigenous Russian diplomacy was the main key to attaining national interests. Invariably, Russian diplomacy focused on maintaining the state's integrity and cultivating its foreign policy opportunities.

This, indeed, is the continuous legacy of more than 1,000 years of Russian history. Since ancient Rus', one of the consistent motivations of the country's foreign policy that has helped shape Russian diplomatic culture has been the urge to engage in the wide range of international relations and to resist the isolation of the Russian nation. This urge was the primary force responsible for creating, developing, and fine-tuning our national diplomatic service. The princes of Rus' married into the royal houses of Europe and Georgia and engaged in commerce and diplomacy from Central Asia to Britain. The Mongol Yoke isolated Russia from Europe but opened up new points of contact in Asia. In the mid-sixteenth century, Russia was presented with new opportunities for rejoining the mainstream of European life. The Holy Roman Empire sent ambassadors to Moscow, while Russian diplomats were frequent visitors to Europe. We continued to have substantive interaction with the East, and Russia turned into an influential power with an active foreign policy.[33] These factors made the creation of a highly organized diplomatic service imperative, and in 1549 the *Posolsky Prikaz* (Foreign Office, literally the Office of Embassies) was established. Its first head was Ivan Mikhailovich Viskovaty, who contributed significantly to the foundation of Russian diplomacy.

During this period, the Office of Embassies began to act as the coordinating center for Russian foreign policy. One of its first directors was Afanasiy Ordin-Nashchokin (1605–81)—considered "the Russian Richelieu" by his contemporaries—who described the office as "the eye of all Great Russia." Ordin-Nashchokin maintained that any progress Russia made abroad would be fleeting unless it was supported by growth and development at home.[34]

A qualitative divide in Russian diplomacy came during the era of Peter the Great (reigned 1682–1725); Russia emerged as a major European power once it had gained permanent access to the Baltic. During his 1697–99 Grand Embassy to Europe, Peter introduced the summit meeting into Russian diplomatic practice, personally negotiating and signing several major treaties.[35]

Peter the Great's innovative approach to foreign policy led to the radical restructuring of diplomatic agencies along collegial lines and stressed the need for professionally trained diplomats. Since that time, Russian diplomacy, under the leadership and direction of the Russian head of state, has organized its work in a collegial fashion. This remains a distinctive characteristic even to this day. The Office of Embassies, which lasted more than 170 years, was transformed in 1720 into the College of Foreign Affairs (*Kollegiya inostrannykh del*). The efforts of the college and of the network of permanent diplomatic missions Peter the Great had established abroad were aimed at preserving the "general quiet in Europe."

Russia's might and influence continued to grow under the reign of Catherine II (reigned 1762–96). Catherine took an energetic and active interest in foreign policy. She was aided by a series of talented advisers and diplomats, including Grigory Potemkin (1739–91), Nikita Panin (1718–83), and Aleksandr Andreevich Bezborodko (1747–99). A crowning achievement of Russian diplomacy was the signing of the Treaty of Kuchuk-Kainarji in 1774, which ended the Russo-Turkish War.[36]

In matters of war and peace, Russian diplomacy was sometimes significantly ahead of its time. For example, in 1804, at the height of the Napoleonic Wars, Alexander I proclaimed that great powers should, in the future, agree to recognize the integrity of each other's borders. After

Napoleon's defeat in 1815, Russia proposed a "one-time, proportional disarmament of European powers." Essentially, this was the first general disarmament initiative in history.

This is Russia's great proclivity then, surfacing everywhere throughout the history of its foreign policy and forming one of the key elements of its continuity: taking the initiative in creating a system of international relations at all stages of its evolution. After Napoleon's defeat, Russia was one of the main participants in creating the new European order (the Concert of Europe, as well as the Holy Alliance). This precedent was imitated after World War II, in attempting to create a European system based on a balance—however delicate—between the primary European powers and the alliances they had formed.

The fact that Russia traditionally lagged behind its leading partners economically stimulated diplomats to seek additional tools for bringing peace and stability to the European continent. One of the most striking examples of this policy was Russia's role in assembling the first Hague Conference of 1899. Its primary goal, according to the note distributed by Foreign Minister M. N. Muraviev, was to "preserve universal peace and reduce as much as possible the weapons that threaten mankind."[37] Although the concert of world powers at the time was unprepared to make actual reductions in weapons or military expenditures, the Hague Conference was essential in creating the conceptual foundation for an international process that would only become fully significant during the second half of the twentieth century, when the urgency of finding a framework for arms control and disarmament was acknowledged by the international community. At The Hague, the European powers for the first time acknowledged—in principle—their desire to reduce military expenditures, and thus opened the way to broad international discussions on disarmament. Another important result of the Hague Conference was the Convention on Laws and Customs of War on Land, which laid the foundation for one of the most dynamically developing areas of modern international law in recent years.

The soul of the Hague Conference was Russia's delegate, Fyodor Martens, a diplomat and authority on international law.[38] Martens's name and legacy have only recently been restored and properly recognized by Russian diplomatic and scholarly communities. In particular,

Martens is remembered for his theory of governing international relations. One modern study of his life and work notes:

He supposed that progressive development of humankind would only lead to increasingly intense communication between states and thus to improved and more stable international governance. International governance was, in his eyes, a real way to eliminate military conflict. If we follow Martens's ideas, then permanent peace on Earth should be attainable through the gradual efforts of international law—to create law and order in the world community commensurate with the achievements of human civilization—and the gradual development of international government—which makes lasting peaceful cooperation between nations possible. According to Martens, this is a slow and complicated process, but the only path that will give the world permanent peace.[39]

It is impossible not to see the relevance of these ideas in today's globalized environment and with our transition from a bipolar to multipolar world order. It is impossible not to see the relevance, when we feel a sharp need for reliable institutions to manage global processes and provide strategic stability in the broadest meaning of the word. And this is yet another indication of how important it is, from a practical standpoint, to restore the historic legacy of Russian diplomacy.

Another valuable tradition of Russian diplomacy is its pragmatism—a sober and realistic view of Russia's place and role in international relations, unencumbered by any ideological prejudices or stereotypes. This can be seen, more specifically, in the relationship of prominent Russian diplomats to the age-old arguments and discussions regarding Russia's geopolitical position and the role of Russian civilization as an intermediary between Europe and Asia. Russian diplomacy never gave credence to the artificial juxtaposition of East and West as two supposedly contradictory vectors for Russian foreign policy. Undoubtedly, beginning with Peter the Great, Russia's diplomacy was oriented first and foremost toward Europe. It was through Europe that Russia was destined to find her place as a world power and acquire the cultural and social riches already produced by Western Europe at the time. Peter's insistence on having a "window to Europe" turned out to be one of the most visionary and productive ideas in the history of Russian foreign policy. By the beginning of the nineteenth century, especially after the destruction of Napoleon, Russia had become an equal—even the leading—power in Europe's concert.

The development of an active European policy was also a great help in realizing Russia's far-reaching interests in the East. In particular, Aleksandr Gorchakov did not limit his activity to Europe, but vigorously pursued the establishment of ties with the "second tier" states at that time, such as China, Japan, the United States, and Brazil. Gorchakov was a proponent of a "multivectored" foreign policy, which has become one of the fundamental elements in Russia's foreign policy concept today.

The traditional European orientation of Russia's diplomacy, however, is important for another reason in the contemporary arena. Russia's deep involvement in Europe's politics, together with its close economic, cultural, and historic ties to Western Europe—developed extensively during the late nineteenth and early twentieth centuries—have never hindered Russian diplomacy in vigorously, even harshly, protecting the country's national interests. Thus, the second half of the nineteenth century was a period of very close cultural exchange between Russia and Western Europe—the same time period in which Russia often stood alone against a powerful coalition of European powers. History fully refutes the idea that an independent Russian foreign policy must unavoidably be accompanied by confrontation with the West or by withdrawal into isolation. The experience of Russian diplomacy in recent years demonstrates the gradual formation of a style of mutual relations that combines the firm defense of national interests with an equally consistent search for mutually acceptable solutions through dialogue and cooperation with the West.

The concept of continuity in foreign policy has not only positive but negative historical contexts as well. In particular, we must examine the "imperial" nature of Russian foreign policy that was prevalent during the eighteenth and nineteenth centuries and that, in a unique interpretation, continued to leave its mark during the Soviet period. It is obvious that the realities of Russia and the Commonwealth of Independent States today demand a deep and comprehensive overhaul of this historical experience, especially with regard to Russia's closest neighbors. In particular, the issue of bilateral ties between Russia and Central and Eastern European states is important. Relations with some of these countries continue to suffer because of our complex, contradictory, and sometimes tragic history. It is the task of modern diplomacy—without glossing over or refuting these negative moments of the past—to work patiently and consistently toward overcoming them and starting anew.

The situation that unfolded in Central Europe after the end of the cold war demonstrates the explosive potential hidden behind mutual historic animosity and international conflicts. One of the proofs of this is the tragedy in the Balkans. The most important thing we can glean from these events is that modern Europe must not be held hostage by its history. Of course, we cannot ignore or hush up past mistakes, omissions, and difficulties. But they should serve as lessons or warnings, and not be used as a means and argument for continuing to support hostility and to complicate bilateral relations.

This is the approach taken by Russian diplomacy toward its relations with several states, most notably Poland. Nevertheless, such political relationships must not be one sided. The healing of historic injuries in bilateral relations demands mutual effort, mutual tact, and respect for national sentiments.

Special consideration is deserved for the historic aspects of ties with former Soviet republics. Here, there is a complex web of ties that bound together Russia and these republics, and both positive and negative experience have accumulated in our historical relationships, connected with the manner in which each of these countries became part of the Russian Empire, and later, of the Soviet Union. In the current transitional stage of relations with the CIS, it is not easy to overcome at once all the difficulties and complexities connected with the combination of natural tendencies toward increased national consciousness on the part of the other new republics and the negative manifestations of nationalism. This objectively complicates the process of jointly crafting long-range priorities and specific directions for cooperation in the realm of foreign policy. We must be prepared for the fact that this process will be arduous and that we will have to take into account not only current factors related to the economy, politics, and culture, but also issues arising out of history.

Issues of continuity should be examined separately in diplomacy, used as a tool of foreign policy. Diplomacy is by definition one of the most "international" aspects of human activity. Unlike foreign policy, which is the prerogative of one nation alone, the birth and development of diplomacy have always been inseparably linked to the establishment of international relations. Despite the diversity of national diplomatic schools and traditions, the general historic tendency in the world has been, and will be, for diplomacy to seek to unify the organizational and technical aspects of the activity of foreign policy in order to attain its primary goal: facilitating mutual understanding between states and harmonizing their shared interests. A colorful example of how diplomacy brings this about are the resolutions adopted at the 1815 Congress of Vienna, which not only defined the system of international relations for Europe, but also regulated its operations. As one of the most active participants of European politics at the time, Russia's diplomatic service developed in close interaction with the diplomatic agencies of the other leading European powers. Indeed, the question of continuity in diplomacy, and of its organization, tools, and methods, cannot be examined in the narrow context of a single nation. It can only be seriously studied within the context of how international relations unfold at the global level.

The fate of Russian diplomacy in the twentieth century, however, emerged dramatically, even tragically, and reflects the zigzags taken by the Russian state throughout the last century. In particular, Russia's diplomatic service has been marked by two difficult defining moments.

The revolution of 1917 created an abrupt break in Russia's diplomatic tradition. The foreign policy establishment—the Ministry of Foreign Affairs, the diplomatic corps, and so on—was practically the only government institution from tsarist Russia of which almost none of the employees stayed on to work for the Bolsheviks. For its part, the Soviet government reacted to perceived "sabotage" in the diplomatic corps by firing all Russian ambassadors and envoys abroad "without pension and without the right to be hired for any government post."[40] It was only several years after the revolution, after career diplomat G. V. Chicherin (1872–1936)[41] was appointed to head the People's Commissariat of

Foreign Affairs (NKID), and after the USSR received formal, de jure diplomatic recognition, that the Soviet school of diplomacy gradually began to take shape. However, even in the ensuing years this process was not smooth or consistent. Stalinist repression in the 1930s dealt an enormous blow to the foreign policy apparatus, because for all intents and purposes an entire generation of Soviet diplomats was liquidated. For those who survived this period, there was a time when wind blew through the empty corridors of the NKID. Nonetheless, the foreign policy service was able in a relatively short period of time to replenish its ranks and restore considerable creativity into Soviet diplomacy, using it to protect the Soviet Union's national interests.

Russia's foreign policy service today objectively continues the best traditions of Soviet diplomacy, but with a broader mission: to restore the historic continuity of a Russian national foreign policy and diplomacy. Not only is this in obligation to the previous generations of Russian diplomats who devoted their talents in service to the interests of our homeland, but it is also in order to use their legacy to shape Russia's modern foreign policy. The diplomatic service is continually incorporating new areas of international relations devoted to solving the widening range of global issues. However, a truly professional and effective foreign policy service is only possible if it rests firmly on history, tradition, and national and cultural values. Respect for the past is what binds the historic process together as a whole. It is also what preserves and magnifies the best traditions of Russian diplomacy. Looking at history allows us to glean lessons for today and tomorrow, to compare old and newly acquired experience, and to correlate with past experience the new and challenging tasks faced by foreign policy in today's ever-changing world.

This is why the cultivation of a sensitive approach to our historic legacy should be obligatory in the education and training of the new generation of Russian diplomats. It is important to inculcate in them the ability to perceive the modern world's development within a broad historic perspective and in relation to the future goals and aspirations of their own country. This is the reference point that will plot a sure course for Russia in international affairs through the current critical period of change, both in our country and in the world community.

Breakfast meeting with Henry Kissinger at the Russian Embassy in Washington, May 20, 2001.

2

THE FORMATION OF A
NEW INTERNATIONAL SYSTEM

After the Cold War

On the threshold of the new century, the struggle has intensified to identify the principles that will guide the international
order and to replace those that held sway in the twentieth century's bipolar world. The end of the cold war offered mankind
an unprecedented opportunity to restructure international
affairs based on fairness and democracy. By the end of the
1980s, the combined efforts of the Soviet Union and the
United States (along with other nations) were able to eliminate the threat of global nuclear war. Building on this new-
found cooperation, they were able to reduce nuclear arsenals,
to strengthen the atmosphere of trust in international relations, and to substantially reduce military tensions in Europe.
Most important, they were able to untie the Gordian knot
posed by German unification. The world community had a
historic opportunity to establish an international order based
on democracy and law and to enter into the twenty-first century free from the confrontational legacy of the past.
Moreover, this could have been done without abandoning the

enormous body of beneficial agreements and treaties that had been crafted in previous eras.

However, this chance was not fully realized. Researchers at the U.S. East-West Institute concluded:

A unique opportunity was lost to use the end of the cold war and fall of communism to further the development of a new world based on agreement between the great powers, on a mature, authoritative and effective United Nations, on the new security architecture in Europe which replaced the old balance between two opposing military alliances, and by encouraging multilateral systems of security in the Far East, in Central and South Asia, and in other regions. The world lost an unprecedented opportunity to make enormous break-throughs in nuclear disarmament and render harmless the cold war's nuclear arsenals, to stop the spread of weapons of mass destruction, to further reduce conventional weapons in Europe and the Far East, and to develop an efficient mechanism to enforce and maintain peace based on the mutual understanding by Russia and the West of resolutions on the use of force, when necessary, and on the joint execution of these resolutions.[1]

What is the explanation for this failure?

One of the reasons is that in the aftermath of the fall of the bipolar system of international relations, the scale of the problems and challenges that arose in its place turned out to be much more serious than anyone could have predicted at the beginning of the 1990s. Indeed, the stability of many states and entire regions was shaken by conflicts caused by interethnic strife, extremism, and aggressive separatism. There was increased danger that those in charge would lose control of nuclear weapons and other weapons of mass destruction. The gulf between the wealthy and the poor countries widened, which in and of itself is a potential source of conflict. The world's ecology and climate continue to be threatened. Mankind is threatened by new diseases. Drug trafficking and organized crime continue to increase unabated.

In an open and interdependent world, these and other threats take on an increasingly transnational nature and affect the security of all states. This is evidenced by the spread of international terrorism, which has become one of the world community's most serious and dangerous challenges. The "terrorist international," which stretches in an arc from the Balkans to the North Caucasus, into Central Asia, and on to the Philippines and Indonesia, threatens to destabilize not only specific states, but also entire regions, and to undermine international security for all.

We must acknowledge that the international community as a whole has proved unable to meet these challenges effectively. Of course, during the past ten years we have gained much experience in constructively solving international problems, some of it in peace-building and conflict-resolution efforts. However, we continue to lack a comprehensive strategy for pursuing peace and security geared to addressing contemporary concerns. It has become increasingly apparent that this problem requires a more systematic approach. The fundamental question for the world community is as follows: what should the future global system be like as a whole?

When the cold war ended, international relations lost the tools that superpower rivalry had provided for conflict management. Yet new mechanisms for ensuring stability in a situation that had changed radically were not created in their place. In the opinion of Adam Rotfeld, director of the Stockholm International Peace Research Institute, "a single organizing principle for global security has not been developed."[2]

Many in the West were—and continue to be—convinced that the wide distribution of democratic values throughout the world and the increasing conversion of countries to liberal market economies are powerful stabilizing factors in international affairs, the so-called democratic peace theory of international relations. An illustration of this viewpoint is the way U.S. specialists at the Pentagon's Institute for National Strategic Studies classify the nations of the world into four groups, depending on the level and stability of their democratic systems: core states, transition states, rogue states, and failing states.[3] According to this scheme, each state is awarded what amounts to a behavior grade, the main determinant of which is how close it approaches the ideal of the American political system.[4]

Meanwhile, it is becoming clear that although the process of democratization is indisputably a positive force, it cannot by itself be seen as the "organizing principle for global security" mentioned earlier. This is evidenced by the nature of the local conflicts going on today around the world. Although the overwhelming majority of these conflicts are internal, their source is not conflict between a democracy and dictatorship. Rather, ethnic or religious animosity, social degradation, or militant separatism motivates these conflicts. Moreover, as experience has shown in some developed European states—Great Britain, France, and Belgium, for example—ethnic and religious conflicts may flare up even in a stable democracy. At best, a democratic system allows these conflicts to be averted and resolved in a civilized way, but it does not eliminate their underlying roots.

Democratization, as such, is not the answer for other international challenges. Indeed, the process of democratization must be protected from such threats as international terrorism and organized crime. Regarding the spread of weapons of mass destruction, experience demonstrates that being a "respectable" democracy does not preclude involvement in regional confrontation or an arms buildup.

All this leads us to conclude that a key issue in international relations today is the nature of the future international system. Will it be multipolar, to accommodate the wide-ranging interests of the global community? Or will the interests of a single nation or group of states dictate it? The answer to this question will determine, to a great extent, mankind's ability to manage international processes and keep international affairs from sliding into chaos.

Meanwhile, the establishment of a new system for international relations has become more complicated and protracted. Foreign analysts struggle to give the current stage in world development a comprehensive determination. Some have dubbed it the "new world dis-order" (Henry Kissinger). Others describe it as "an amorphous system of security lacking the bipolar structure and ideological clarity of the cold war."[5] There are those who predict that the present "uncertainty" of the international system will continue for many decades. Various scenarios are suggested, ranging from a new era of globalization and universal prosperity at one end, to the collapse of international affairs into complete anarchy, at the other.

One fact is above dispute: the international system finds itself in a transitional state and its future will be determined by the political will demonstrated by the world community. It is the world community that must set the parameters of the international system and construct reliable institutions to ensure safety and stability in international relations. The shaping of a new world order demands a conscious, focused effort by all nations. The acceptance of "naturally occurring" globalization through passivity or out of national egotism, or worse, a return to competition and pursuing individual interests at the expense of others, will only lead to negative tendencies that the world community will have more and more difficulty controlling.

Unfortunately, there is as yet no conceptual unity on this vital global issue. Moreover, two fundamentally opposed approaches to a new international system have come into competition in recent years. One of them advocates a one-size-fits-all model. In this model, the international arena is dominated by a group of more-developed countries, enjoying the military and economic support of the United States and NATO, while the rest of the world community must live according to rules established and, occasionally, enforced by this elite club. An example of this model in action was the fate of Yugoslavia, particularly in 1999.

The roots of this model run deep and are cemented, as was pointed out earlier, in a mistaken analysis of the international changes that occurred in the late 1980s and early 1990s. French foreign affairs minister Hubert Védrine has acknowledged that "considering itself to have been victorious in the Third World War (that is, the cold war), the West has come to believe it has unlimited opportunities and, because of its technological superiority, sees no reason not to impose its beliefs everywhere."[6] Seemingly at odds with their own advocacy of democracy for everyone in the world, the United States and its allies, according to the apt observation of former UNESCO director-general Federico Mayor, have begun to "act as an oligarchy in addressing transnational issues."[7]

A logical consequence of this one-sided approach has been the gradual revision of the principles of democracy and consensus within the international system that seemed ready to gain ground after the fall of the Berlin Wall. The idea of building a unified Europe gradually gave way to "NATO-centrism" and an attempt to forge European security based on only a single, closed military and political alliance. Not only did NATO expand eastward, it adopted a new strategy which called for expanding its sphere of influence beyond the limits established by the North Atlantic Treaty. Moreover, NATO has undertaken military action unsanctioned by the UN Security Council, that is, in violation of the UN Charter and the founding principles of international law.[8]

As a kind of test case for the development of this NATO-centric concept for European security, NATO deployed military forces against Yugoslavia, which precipitated an extremely serious international crisis in the post–cold war period, with well-known results. The 1999 military action in Yugoslavia dealt a serious blow to the foundations of international law and order and to stability. Once again, the military aspects of world security came to the forefront. A number of countries began to announce that engaging in massive arms buildups was the only way to prevent foreign aggression. As a result, this changed climate in international affairs represents a further threat to the existing regimes that are intended to prevent the proliferation of weapons of mass destruction and their delivery systems (such as ballistic missiles).

In the West today, these facts are forcing an unwilling reexamination of this unlawful action against Yugoslavia. Thankfully, the conclusion is being reached that it cannot serve as a model for such actions by the alliance in the future.[9] Russia perceived the error of NATO's course of action from the outset. Everything that Russian diplomacy warned about during the struggle to avert NATO's aggression has unfortunately come to pass. Not only did armed interference fail to solve a single one of the problems festering in the Balkans, but intervention has created a deadlock that can only be resolved at an enormous diplomatic price. Ultimately, the NATO operation produced new suffering for the peaceful population of Kosovo, in place of the suffering it was undertaken to eliminate.

Both staying out of the conflict and engaging NATO in the conflict were equally unacceptable choices for Russia. Russian diplomacy took a constructive approach, helping to end the aggression and encourage a political resolution to the problem of Yugoslavia, as outlined in UN Security Council resolution 1244.[10]

The crisis in the Balkans raised several important issues for the world community. To justify NATO's actions, the West began to vigorously tout the concepts of "humanitarian intervention" and "limited sovereignty." Attempts have continued to try and impose this thesis: that in defense of human rights and to avert humanitarian disaster, it is permissible to use force against a sovereign nation, unsanctioned by the UN Security Council.

It goes without question that the world community cannot and should not stand idly by when there are flagrant violations of human rights, especially when national or ethnic suffering ensues. In addition, humanitarian crises can make it considerably more complicated to maintain regional and international stability. However, it is impermissible to counter human rights violations with methods that commit the same violations. Disregard for the principles of sovereignty and the territorial integrity of states, both embodied in Article 2 of the UN Charter, is a fundamental threat to international stability.

At the heart of the concept of humanitarian intervention lies the false notion that with globalization the role of a state as a subject of international relations is unavoidably reduced to nothing. Yet Russia's experience, and the experience of several other countries that have undertaken democratic reforms, dictates the opposite: namely, that the weakening of the state's authority leads to the spread of such phenomena as international terrorism, militant separatism, and organized crime. This is why, in working to strengthen its democratic state system, its sovereignty, and its territorial integrity, Russia acts not only in its own interests, but also, in the long run, in the interests of global stability and security.

Against the backdrop of an intensified struggle over fundamental issues of global development, the model of a multilateral world system proposed by Russia is increasingly appealing. This model proposes a central role for *collective* mechanisms to support peace and security, held together by the principles of international law and equal security for all states. This proposal was succinctly expressed in Russia's 1999 Concept for Peace in the Twenty-First Century, a code of values and principles for relations between states designed to uphold international law and order without war or violence. This Concept was submitted by Russia as part of the preparation for the UN's Millennium Assembly (held in New York in September 2000).

The idea of a multilateral world is not a speculative slogan, but rather a philosophy for international activity based on the realities of globalization today. As specialists from many countries acknowledge, we already live in a multilateral world. Today, no one country or group of countries has the resources necessary to impose its will unilaterally in a world where all other states enjoy only "limited sovereignty." Specifically, neither the United States nor NATO is in a position to ensure international security alone, playing the role of global policeman.

A clear example of this is the significant worsening of the Middle East crisis during 2000–01. Dramatic events in this region have once again shown that in an age of globalization, no one single state, regardless of how powerful or influential it may be, is able to single-handedly manage a regional situation, much less processes on a global scale. Ensuring stability and regulating conflict require the collective efforts of the entire world community. Moreover, centers of economic and political influence other than the United States and Western Europe should play a role in global policy, including Russia, China, India, Japan, and the Muslim world. Meanwhile, forces for unification and integration are gaining momentum in Southeast Asia, Latin America, and Africa. In general, the greater the level of economic integration in these areas, the stronger the tendency to establish a collective position on international issues and to carry out a coordinated foreign policy.

According to American political analyst Samuel Huntington, the present orientation of U.S. policy toward a unipolar world is counterproductive and conflicts with the world community's interests. "The United States," he writes,

> would clearly prefer a unipolar system in which it would be the hegemon and often acts as if such a system existed. The major powers, on the other hand, would prefer a multipolar system in which they could pursue their interests, unilaterally and collectively, without being subject to constraints, coercion, and pressure by the stronger superpower. They feel threatened by what they see as the American pursuit of global hegemony.[11]

Some Russian analysts see any attempt to create multipolarity as uneconomical, given Russia's limited resources. They also feel that "to a certain extent it deprives Russia of its independence, almost automatically drawing Russia into opposition with the United States and sometimes with the West as a whole."[12] It is difficult to agree with this position. Our choice in favor of a multipolar world system is conditioned above all on our national interests. It is within the framework of a system based on collective global security that Russia has the best chance of finding its deserved place among the world community.

The concept of multipolarity is not promoted in abstract discussions, but as part of the process of seeking joint solutions to the most serious and complex international issues, issues that directly affect Russia's vital interests. These issues are ensuring strategic stability, regulating local conflicts under the auspices of the UN, and establishing an overarching, unified system of security for Europe. It is diplomatic efforts toward the fair resolution of these issues that lay the foundation for a multipolar international system.

The line endorsed by Russia, which both vigorously defends our national interests and actively seeks mutually acceptable solutions to disputed issues, does not predestine Russia to oppose the West. The facts demonstrate just the opposite. In the UN Security Council, Russia achieves consensus with the other permanent members of this body (the United States, Great Britain, France, and China) on the majority of issues, which makes possible constructive solutions that are in the interests of the world community. Moreover, the multilateral format of international organizations and forums makes it possible for Russian diplomacy to actively create a wide circle of supporters for our conceptual approaches to the issues.

The struggle to create a multipolar world system, therefore, does not involve opposition, but is instead a strategy of successive steps toward a new architecture of international relations. One of the main directions of this strategy is for the world community to develop a method of crafting collective responses to the challenges posed by the modern world. While the prominent feature of the twentieth century may have been our fight to stave off nuclear disaster, the tasks we face today are much more diverse and complex. Above all, we must ensure humanity's continued progress by providing reliable security for all, by using technological advances for the good of the entire world community, and by reducing the developmental disparities among nations.

This goal requires effective institutions to regulate international processes. These mechanisms should guarantee the equal participation of all nations in international affairs and allow for an equal contribution by all to solving global problems. The more nations that participate in the process, the stronger an international agreement will be in a given area, and thus, the international system as a whole will be sturdier.

The new architecture of international security should correspond to the multipolarity of today's world. The three building materials for this architecture are essentially already in place. They are a well-developed system of international organizations headed by the United Nations, influential regional groupings, and the tightly woven fabric of bilateral relations between states. The challenge is to turn these elements into an integrated system that will mesh the needs of individual states with the interests of the entire global community.

A central place in this array belongs to the UN, as the linchpin of a multipolar world system, as well as to other global institutions and forums: UNESCO, the World Health Organization, the International Agency for Atomic Energy, and so on. The next link is formed by regional and subregional organizations. The development of integrated processes in various regions of the world is a prominent tendency today. As French president Jacques Chirac noted,

> to better organize the international system in the twenty-first century, it will above all be necessary to move toward a multipolar world. As a reaction to globalization, most states will opt to form mutual unions at the regional level so that they may remain masters of their own fate. The European Union is the most advanced example of this need for regional integration.[13]

Developments taking place in Europe, especially the construction of a new European architecture, have wider significance. For centuries, Europe was the center of international affairs. It was the primary legislator of international principles and standards. Military-political coalitions and unions rose and fell in Europe, and their clashes produced some of the bloodiest wars in history. Today, Europe represents, in miniature, the diversity and real multipolarity of the world. Therefore, we can expect that the system of security Europe develops for itself will in many ways influence the future world system as a whole.

An example of the continually increasing importance of regional factors in global politics is the unprecedented process of integration that has unfolded in recent years in Asia and the Pacific. This integration has been accompanied by an active search for reliable ways to ensure security in the region and to develop political dialogue between Asian governments and the world's other primary poles of influence. In addition to strengthening the main structure integrating the countries of the Pacific Basin—the Asia-Pacific Economic Cooperation (APEC) forum—the region has developed international channels of political dialogue like the ASEAN regional forum and has established institutions for ongoing joint work such as the Asia-Europe Meeting (ASEM) and others. The Shanghai Cooperation Organization, founded in June 2001, has a particularly good chance of success, and the notion of a true pan-Asian dialogue (stretching from the Middle East to the Russian Far East) is being advanced in the form of CICA (the Conference on Interaction and Confidence-Building Measures in Asia).

A world network of regional organizations includes the dynamically evolving structures of economic integration and political cooperation that unite countries in the Arab world, in Latin America, and in Africa. Evidence that these structures will play a growing role is evidenced by the creation in mid-2001 of the African Union.

Finally, the third element of a new international system is the dense network of bilateral relations between states that define everything from security cooperation to trade. This natural and traditional form of interaction between states is as important as it ever was in today's globalized environment.

Thus, the future global architecture can be seen as a kind of pyramid, with the top position held by the United Nations, as the primary instrument for maintaining peace and security, whose actions are supplemented by cooperation promoted by regional organizations and through direct bilateral relations. The binding force of this system would be grounded in the universal jurisdiction of and strict adherence to international law.

The evolution of the international system undoubtedly requires some adaptation of international legal standards to the new reality. In particular, it is necessary to give the world community the wherewithal to more effectively and smoothly react to—or better yet, to avert—humanitarian crises. Efforts to achieve this should be conducted collectively and only within the framework of the United Nations. No one has the right to ignore the fact that all available instruments of international humanitarian law spell out the appropriate reaction to the violation of corresponding standards, right up to and including turning the situation over to the UN Security Council. This procedure, established in numerous multilateral conventions and treaties, is obligatory if a situation seems to warrant the imposition of measures in response to a humanitarian crisis. An initiative introduced by Russia in the UN calls for the collective clarification of the legal aspects of the international use of force in the current situation of globalization. Serious study should also be devoted to developing preventive diplomacy and peace-making practices, and to improving the use of sanctions.

A recent source of regional and international tension, and an extremely serious problem from the point of view of international law, is the approach of the United States to the so-called rogue states, against which a virtual undeclared war is being levied. Unilateral sanctions and trade embargoes are being used, as is political and military pressure—up to and including the use of military force, as in previous situations with Iraq and Yugoslavia. This cannot disguise the fact that the internal affairs of sovereign states are being interfered with.

The counterproductivity of this line of action is beyond question. In not a single instance has the United States has been able to bring about the overthrow of a government it dislikes through the imposition of harsh sanctions, and the true victims of sanctions (and the air campaigns) have been the peaceful populations. It is worth noting that Washington seems finally to have begun to realize this, at least in certain cases.

Russia's position in the matter of states accused by the international community of human rights violations, or other violations of international law, is clear and consistent. Forceful means of pressure may be brought to bear, including sanctions by the world community, but should only be applied with great consideration and caution. We must take care that the cure is not worse than the illness. It is essential that no state, no matter how critical the situation within its borders or around it, should feel itself backed into a corner or that its security is being threatened. No matter what the circumstances, such states should be given viable alternatives that bring them out of isolation and into positive participation in regional security and international affairs. An example of this principle in action are Russia's efforts to aid in regulating the situation on the Korean Peninsula. Russia works to support national reconciliation between North and South Korea.

In general, one of the basic principles of the new international system should be the maximum involvement of all nations in joint efforts to ensure security and stability. Only with the involvement of all nations can we attain the critical mass of multilateral diplomacy, which produces the international environment needed for the political management of current conflicts and the prevention of new ones. Events have shown that Russia's position regarding a new international system enjoys growing support. When Russia, China, and India—representing half the world's population—firmly denounced NATO's action against Yugoslavia in March 1999 and warned against the extremely destructive results of "humanitarian intervention," our voices were heard and influenced the position of other UN members. As a result there is a growing, unified, international front in defense of the UN Charter's founding principles. The final documents of the Thirteenth Ministerial Conference of the Movement of the Non-Aligned Countries (Cartageña, April 8–9, 2000) and the South Summit of the Group of 77 (Havana, April 10–14, 2000) state: "We reject the so-called 'right' of humanitarian intervention, which has no legal basis in the UN Charter or in the general principles of international law."[14] In Cartageña the Non-Aligned Movement also unanimously expressed its "firm condemnation of all unilateral military actions including those made without proper authorization from the United Nations Security Council."[15]

The Challenge of Globalization

One dramatic effect of the end of the cold war was to make modern international relations much more open. Barriers were destroyed, and the artificial division of the world into closed blocs was eliminated. Development models based on isolation and autarky were fully discredited. The transition of the majority of states to open market economies and the liberalization of world economics and trade were a quantum leap in the transformation of the world into a unified economic and civilized space.

At the same time, globalization received enormous stimulus in all areas of human endeavor and became the most important factor in world development for the twenty-first century. Today, no serious medium-range analysis of development in Russia or in the world is possible without taking into account the effects of globalization, and certainly no long-range forecasting.

Yet scholars and specialists do not agree on the essential characteristics of globalization, and the term continues to elude any precise definition. Some consider globalization to be a completely new phenomenon, related primarily to the scientific and technical revolution and also to the unprecedented growth of transnational finance, the volume of which exceeds what is accrued from production and international trade many times over. Others assert that globalization is simply the next stage in the process of internationalism, which began at the turn of the nineteenth century but was interrupted by two world wars and the division of the world into two opposing socioeconomic systems. Specialists at the International Monetary Fund define globalization as "the growing economic interdependence of countries worldwide through the increasing volume and variety of cross-border transactions in goods and services and of international capital flows, and also through the more rapid and widespread diffusion of technology."[16]

No matter how we understand globalization, one thing is certain: it is having a more and more noticeable effect on all areas of human activity. It is responsible for the greater internationalization of human affairs and for the growth of interdependence among nations. Yet the real effects of globalization are not uniform.

It would seem that as globalization causes distances between countries and regions to diminish, it should also create a powerful motivation to resolve the world's problems through broad international cooperation. Previously unimaginable opportunities arose to make swift progress toward establishing a new world order based on equal security, joint responsibility, and international cooperation. In the early 1990s Russia, along with the rest of the world, had hopes that the decades of nuclear standoff and global confrontation would be followed by an era of universal peace, security, disarmament, and constructive partnership.

Similarly rosy expectations existed for the resolution of mankind's most vexing problems. Modern technology, it seemed, had the potential to help find optimal solutions for environmental problems, poverty, disease, illiteracy, access to education and culture, and so on. In reality, only a handful of more developed countries have enjoyed any positive effect from globalization. All members of the world community, on the other hand, experience its negative effects to varying degrees.

There is growing evidence that the process of globalization, as it accelerates unchecked by any actions of the international community, is responsible, contrary to the claims made by its proponents, for increasing the gap between rich and poor, both within individual countries and in the world as a whole. According to the 1999 UN report *Globalization with a Human Face,* the income gap between the fifth of the world's people living in the richest countries and the fifth in the poorest was 30 to 1 in 1960. By 1990 it had reached 60 to 1, and by 1997, the ratio stood at 74 to 1.

One of the paradoxes of globalization is that the communications revolution, as manifested especially by the Internet, satellite communications, and mobile telephones, that theoretically should have brought people and countries closer together, is actually making their separation more and more distinct. This is what is referred to as the "digital divide," and the result is that it is the more developed countries that, by and large, can take advantage of the new and unprecedented opportunities for exchanging knowledge and technology.

One effect of globalization that has disturbed many countries is the excessive "economization" of international relations. Economization permits unregulated market forces to dominate the decisionmaking process, somewhat to the exclusion of traditional political and social forces. Moral, ethical, or humanitarian considerations are therefore largely disregarded in the decisionmaking process. There is growing alarm that states and peoples have lost control of their own fates to vaguely defined national market mechanisms and international financial structures that are essentially beyond the citizens' control. The financial crisis that engulfed the world in 1998 and struck so hard at Russia is a clear example of how vulnerable globalization makes the economic security of nations and entire regions.

A sports analogy is often used to compare globalization to a competitive race, in which the winner takes everything and the loser is expected to disappear to the side. The French military journal *Défense Nationale* noted that

the unrestrained economic liberalism so highly touted by the United States (although the United States itself does not follow it) is responsible for widening the gap between the developed and the developing countries. This inequality and unfairness engenders a resentment that feeds rebellion and terrorism in developing countries. The pursuit of profit as a guiding principle in human endeavor leads to moral degradation and suicidal "drift."[17]

An alarming symptom of the situation is that as the poorest countries fall farther and farther behind, they generally receive decreasing amounts of international aid for their development needs. The problematic sociology of developing countries receives less and less attention, as only one thing is demanded from them—that they carry out liberal market reforms. Yet it is well understood that this does not guarantee an influx of foreign investment. On the contrary, the lion's share of capital investment goes to the same group of developed countries.

As a result, instead of a shared space where countries can flourish economically, there is only a shared "space" of poverty and social degradation, which fosters the modern challenges of international terrorism and organized crime, the trade in illegal drugs and arms, and national and religious intolerance. And these problems often grow at a much faster rate than does internationalization in the fields that would most help: health care, education, science, and culture. This trend was noted by UN under-secretary-general Pino Arlacchi: "Never before has there been so much economic opportunity for so many people. And never before has there been so much opportunity for criminal organizations to exploit the system."[18] It is also apparent that globalization has not helped the world community more effectively address mankind's long-range problems, such as ecological and industrial disasters and epidemic disease. On the contrary, the constraints imposed today by the free market trends mentioned earlier make it all the more difficult to deal effectively with global issues like these.

Finally, the paradox of globalization insinuates itself into intellectual and cultural life with greater and greater effect. New means of communication, such as the Internet, have provided unique opportunities for mutually enriching exchange in the arts, in education, and in scientific research. Interdependence and cross-border diffusion dominate on the cultural front. Yet, here too we are increasingly aware of the side effects and shortcomings of globalization. Many countries, including Russia, are sounding the alarm against homogenization, against the loss of cultural diversity, and the disappearance of many indigenous languages. Balzac called culture a "nation's clothes," and to further the analogy, the world may soon find itself dressed in the uniform of Americanized mass culture. In various countries—developed as well as developing—international forums are treating the preservation of cultural diversity as seriously as other critical global issues. Within the world community, a consensus is taking shape that cultural diversity is as important for the future of mankind as ecological balance. Globalization should mean greater cultural enrichment between countries, and should not result in the domination of any single culture over the others.

Obviously, an international system based on such striking inconsistencies and contradictions can never be stable. Globalization makes it increasingly difficult for the developed "North" to barricade itself off from the less-developed "South," to create a closed zone where the economy can flourish. Mass immigration into the developed countries of Europe and North America strains the social institutions of these regions. Conversely, the brain drain and exodus of skilled workers seriously hurts the already weakened economies of developing countries.

One of the most complex issues raised by globalization is determining what the proper role of sovereign states should be in international relations. Take, for example, the phenomena of militant nationalism and separatism. Guided by an extreme interpretation of the right of nations to self-determination, separatists destroy multiethnic states from the inside out, sowing ethnic hate and intolerance and creating breeding grounds for interethnic conflict that is difficult to manage or control. Separatist movements are hardly restricted to unstable or economically disadvantaged states—they find fertile soil in developed countries as well. This creates a chronic need for the international community to develop proven approaches to such issues as national sovereignty and territorial integrity, the right of ethnic groups to self-determination, minority rights, and so on. There is a need for cooperative solutions that do not permit double standards and the precedents they would engender, with dangerous consequences.

However, the institution of government faces other, more insidious threats. Some of globalization's most wholehearted advocates see government as an anachronism, destined to become extinct. They call for a shift of priority in international affairs, away from the security of states in favor of security for the individual. Yet they remain silent on the question as to who, other than the government of a sovereign state, will guarantee this security. Some assert that the principle of human rights should take absolute precedence over the principles of nonintervention in internal affairs of states and the equal sovereignty of states in international relations.

This is the origin of the concepts of limited sovereignty and humanitarian intervention, discussed above. They are both based on a false supposition: that the institution of government is in and of itself a deterrent to ensuring human rights across the globe. Nevertheless, during recent decades there have been many concrete examples that demonstrate just the opposite. Weakened governments, and in some cases the complete disintegration of governments (the phenomenon of the so-called failed state), have led to conditions of internal chaos and anarchy that left societies not only unable to prevent wholesale human rights violations, but without any means to manage the conflict in their countries.

We must conclude that no matter how many nongovernmental actors take part in international relations today, sovereign states must continue to play the main roles. Even if there are calls to focus international cooperative efforts on the individual, to concentrate world attention on the interests of personal security, well-being, and dignity, the final responsibility for ensuring such efforts can only rest with governments at the state level. This is, after all, essentially the reason why government was created in the first place.

Of course, we must admit that, especially within the developed countries, a distinct redistribution of function between government and civil society is taking place today—generally in favor of the latter. There is a somewhat similar trend in international relations. More and more issues previously within the purview only of national governments are being debated and addressed at an international level. In particular, the issue of ensuring human rights is no longer considered to be a domestic matter for governments. Nonintervention in a government's internal affairs is increasingly tied to the transparency of government policies on human rights and the level of voluntary cooperation those governments maintain with international bodies. The operative phrase here is "voluntary cooperation." This is not to say that state sovereignty is being eroded, as such, but that the international community is taking a more refined and highly evolved approach to it. Clearly, this process can only occur when all parties are recognized as equals, that is to say, by virtue of—not in spite of—absolute adherence to standards of international law. Sovereign equality is the very principle that allows governments to exercise free will and to cooperate with the world community.

Nevertheless, the doctrines of humanitarian intervention and limited sovereignty deliberately presuppose inequality and a double standard among states. It is clear that these doctrines are not designed to be used against wealthier or militarily stronger countries. They are all about attempting to create an international system in which states' economic inequality—worsening all by itself—would be reinforced by legalized inequality in international relations as well. We would be left with a situation like that described by George Orwell in *Animal Farm:* all are created equal, but some are more equal than others.

In summary, globalization in its present form has not become a new force for regulating international affairs. To the contrary, globalization adds elements of disorganization to the system of international relations and, accordingly, must be closely and carefully managed and controlled for the benefit of the international community.

In soberly evaluating globalization's shortcomings, we must not get carried away. Globalization is an objective and, judging from experience, irreversible process. Trying to outlaw or halt it, as some belligerent social groups in several countries have tried to do, is as senseless as, for example, trying to invalidate scientific discoveries, even if they have the potential to seriously threaten mankind. It is a different matter altogether that the world community can and should try to exert reasonable control over the process of globalization to keep social and humanitarian concerns in the forefront and to lend it some "civility." The voices calling for this approach are more insistent across the globe, from both developing and developed countries alike.

Russia is entirely sympathetic to this approach. Given its current economic situation, Russia is one of those states for whom globalization holds many dangers. No matter what those dangers may be, however, Russia cannot alter its strategic course toward economic openness and full integration into the world economy. It is the task of foreign policy to help this process along by aiding in the establishment of international mechanisms fostering the stable, crisis-free development of Russia's economy. Foreign policy must also work to integrate Russia organically into the world economy, yet minimize our own economic risk.

In his welcome message to the participants of the April 2000 Group of 77 summit meeting in Havana, Russian president Vladimir Putin said, "More important than simply working to limit globalization's negative effects, we must do everything in our power to allow the entire world to reap its benefits. Globalization should serve the cause of social progress, reducing unemployment and eliminating poverty." The world community still needs to learn to manage the dynamics of international interaction and this will certainly not be easy, especially in the area of finance and economics. At the same time, there is a powerful force in the world that counteracts globalization's destructive aspects: the process of regional integration that is spreading vigorously throughout the globe, from Southeast Asia to Latin America.

We have a reliable safety net at our disposal in the area of international relations. In order to be effective, however, it requires clear political will to build a democratic and fair system of international relations, in which states participate based on solidarity, and in which the advocacy of legitimate national interests is balanced by the collective search for mutually acceptable solutions to the world's most serious problems. In short, much remains to be done to transform globalization into a socially responsible force. This will require a comprehensive joint strategy for sustained development and prosperity, based on principles of universal strategic security.

Russia and the Question of Strategic Stability

The profound transformation of international relations in the early 1990s has forced a radical reassessment of the issues surrounding global security and stability. The end of the cold war eliminated the rigorous discipline provided by two opposing military and political blocs and deprived the world of the guiding principles that had shaped international relations for nearly half a century. The world had mended its ideological split, but it did not become any more stable. It faced new threats and challenges to global security, mentioned above: regional conflict, aggressive separatism, interethnic hostility, international terrorism, and organized crime.

Globalization makes it impossible to effectively counter these challenges unless the entire international community works together. Yet cooperative efforts, in turn, are only possible when international relations are stable and predictable, especially between nuclear powers.

Of all the considerable significant international relations successes in the second half of the twentieth century, none was more important for mankind's future than eliminating the threat of nuclear annihilation. The joint efforts of Russia and the United States (along with other powers) brought the threat to zero and even began a process of limiting and reducing nuclear arsenals. This was achieved through universal acceptance of the concept of strategic stability. Its cornerstone was the 1972 Anti-Ballistic Missile Treaty.[19]

The key to the strategic stability established by the ABM Treaty lies in the conscious mutual rejection by its signatories of strategic defense systems as effective protection from intercontinental ballistic missiles (ICBMs). It was the rejection of such defense systems that eliminated the need for Russia and the United States to continue to amass offensive nuclear potential and allowed the two countries to engage in a policy of mutual restraint with reduced levels of strategic arms. In other words, by rejecting a nuclear shield, the nuclear sword was made less dangerous.[20]

The ABM Treaty was the foundation for an entire network of international treaties and agreements on arms control and disarmament. These included SALT I (1972) and SALT II (1979), as well as the INF Treaty (1987), which eliminated two entire classes of nuclear weapons systems—intermediate-range and shorter-range missiles. These were followed by START I (1991) and START II (1993), which aim to reduce the total number of nuclear warheads by more than 75 percent. There continue to be very real opportunities for further and deeper reduction in offensive strategic weapons.

This adoption of these treaties cannot be separated from both regional and indeed global progress made toward controlling and eliminating weapons of mass destruction (WMD). The bilateral arms control framework helped to engender a number of multilateral treaties, including ones which banned nuclear testing (the Limited Test Ban Treaty was signed in 1963 and the Comprehensive Test Ban Treaty was initialed in 1996). Progress has been made toward nuclear nonproliferation (the initial Non-Proliferation Treaty was concluded in 1968), the elimination of other weapons of mass destruction (the 1990 U.S.-Soviet agreement on ending production of chemical weapons helped to lay the groundwork for the 1993 Chemical Weapons Convention), and efforts to reduce the stockpiles of conventional arms and the size of armed forces.

All of these treaties and agreements helped to create today's architecture for international security and their significance as mutual agreements must be emphasized. If their mutual foundation is destroyed, the entire framework threatens to collapse and take with it the results of the international community's thirty-year effort at disarmament. This is why the entire world has always been so seriously concerned when the United States has made public statements regarding the creation of a strategic missile defense system that violates the ABM Treaty. During the Clinton administration these plans called for a "theater" and then a national missile defense system, while the Bush administration calls for a global defense system.

Russia's firm position against American plans for global antiballistic missile defense does not originate from any lingering competition between superpowers, as was the case when harsh polemics were hurled back and forth between the USSR and the United States on the topic of President Reagan's Strategic Defense Initiative. Russian-American relations have changed dramatically since then, and our governments no longer see each other as adversaries. Moreover, both our countries face largely the same threats and challenges to our security, for example, the spread of weapons of mass destruction, as well as the means for their delivery. Russia is no less interested than the United States and other countries in finding effective solutions to these challenges. However, we are convinced that this must be accomplished together, or at the very least, without negatively impacting the interests of others.

This is why Russia is discussing the issue of strategic stability with the United States not as an adversary intent on any unilateral benefit, but with the goal of finding balanced and well-thought-out solutions. These solutions must, on one hand, reliably ensure the security of our two countries and international strategic stability as a whole, and on the other hand, preserve and further enhance the positive relationship that Russia and the United States have built in recent years.

Throughout 2001, the future of the ABM Treaty was the central topic in the Russian-American dialogue on issues concerning strategic stability and was discussed in depth at the last four meetings between the Russian and American presidents. Russia's position on the issue has been as clear and as constructive as possible: the ABM Treaty remains as valid now as it ever was. Moreover, we have been prepared to pay careful attention to any possible U.S. concerns as a result of the changes that have occurred in the world. We have also been ready to develop a new framework for strategic cooperation. That said, we are governed in our policymaking by the paramount interest of guaranteeing our own security. In so doing, Russia continues to hold the position that we must preserve the multilateral international legal system developed over the past ten years to manage disarmament and arms control. Undermining this system could have grave consequences for the strategic stability of the entire world.

Unfortunately, the U.S. administration preferred to exercise its right to withdraw unilaterally from the ABM Treaty (as provided for under article 15). President Bush officially announced this decision on December 13, 2001. The stated basis for this decision—the threat of nuclear attack by so-called rogue states—remains unconvincing to us. The decision was politically motivated and reflects the exclusive interests of the United States.

The discussions on creating the ABM Treaty and discussions on whether or not to scrap it can hardly be characterized as analytical. The ABM Treaty consists mainly of bans on deploying antiballistic missile defense systems to defend a country's territory and on developing the basis for such a defense (articles 1–8). Waiving this ban would be changing a minus sign to a plus, that is, it would completely eliminate the treaty's purpose.

Another key article in the treaty called for continued talks on limiting strategic offensive weapons (article 11). Rendering the treaty impotent here too directly threatens to destroy the existing system of arms control agreements. Therefore, in accordance with the announcement made at the signing of START I,[21] Russia views the U.S. withdrawal from, or any essential violation of, the ABM Treaty as an exceptional condition allowing Russia to withdraw from START I. Essentially, Russia's withdrawal from the treaty is mandated by the legislation of the Federal Assembly, which ratified START II.[22] Obviously, preparations for START III are directly affected. Thus, even formally, the U.S. unilateral withdrawal from the ABM Treaty called the whole process of nuclear disarmament into question.

Recently, one has been hearing in Washington how the world is different today, and therefore how we can dispense with the whole system of disarmament treaties as long as we are taking good faith unilateral or parallel steps toward reductions in arms. Yet a logical question is immediately raised: are not these efforts motivated by a desire for military and technological superiority that lies beyond any kind of external control? The vital need for external controls is demonstrated by U.S. violations of START I—a treaty that provides for verification measures.[23] What might happen when external control is completely lacking?

The concern of Russia and of other countries in this regard is not a mere formality. The world is seeing more and more clearly that the fight to preserve strategic stability is not Russia's fight alone, but that of the entire international community. If the genie of a new arms race is let out of the bottle, it will not be a response to external threats. Rather, the interests of the military-industrial complex and the development of military technology will dictate the rules of the game. More to the point, it will be a game without rules. This is not so extreme a position if we remember the Soviet-American nuclear arms race of the 1970s and 1980s.

This is why Russia has spoken out for preserving and strengthening the ABM Treaty. In practice, the treaty has proved its central role in preserving strategic stability; it allowed us to seek and to find effective solutions to problems related to the spread of weapons of mass destruction and missile technology. Of course, Russia remains amenable to a joint evaluation of the "new missile threats" raised by our American partners. However, our analysis shows that these threats are hypothetical today. In any case, they are hardly serious enough to jettison the basis of our current strategic stability.

Different technical specialists agree that none of the so-called rogue states possesses missiles capable of striking the United States. Nor will they have this capability in the foreseeable future. The possibility that they may carry out a type of "missile blackmail" against the United States is doubtful. Even less conceivable is the possibilitiy that they might employ ICBMs in a direct attack against the United States. The missile programs of these states are regional in nature. Indeed, rather than states, it would be more useful to speak of "problem regions," where the probability of military conflict is high. If this is so, the management of crisis situations in these regions requires a completely different effort, political and diplomatic, rather than the construction of a missile defense system.

Simply put, the deployment of a strategic antiballistic missile defense system has the potential to seriously destabilize an already fragile system of international security. It is not just a matter of Russian-American strategic relations. It can be predicted that certain countries—for example, China—will take corresponding countermeasures. And an escalation of the arms race in South Asia and in other regions is a possibility that cannot be excluded.

It is easy to imagine what a blow this situation strikes at the policies and process of nuclear nonproliferation. At the Spring 2000 Non-Proliferation Treaty Review Conference, held in New York, many states unanimously spoke out for energetic measures in nuclear arms reduction. They saw this as essential for maintaining a strong NPT. Any attempt to block nuclear arms reduction—which, as we have seen, is closely linked to the future of the ABM Treaty—would likely have a boomerang effect on the Non-Proliferation Treaty. Several states, echoing U.S. rhetoric regarding the ABM Treaty, are already claiming that the NPT has outlived its usefulness and needs reevaluation.

Clearly, an atmosphere such as this makes it practically impossible to exert any restraining influence on the so-called rogue states. On the contrary, increased regional and international instability would essentially stimulate the arms race to expand in various directions, including some which, thankfully, as yet exist only hypothetically. For example, military analysts are already aware of the dangers posed by the production and use of nonmissile technology—so-called suitcase bombs—as delivery systems for weapons of mass destruction. Such weapons could be secretly delivered by terrorists to a foreign territory, without drawing a retaliatory attack and without needing to evade any antiballistic missile defense. Thus, no matter how this issue is approached, it is clear that a global antiballistic missile defense system is an ineffective response to the threat of missile attack. It is also capable of spawning new problems for world security, including the security of the United States.

Although Russia actively works to maintain and strengthen strategic stability, we do not seek to minimize the seriousness of missile proliferation. Russia's position is that the problem requires a fundamentally new, "nondestructive" approach. It is most important to acknowledge that missile proliferation is not a cause but an effect of the more serious global challenges we face. In other words, we must treat the disease, not just its symptoms. First and foremost, this requires effective political and diplomatic ways to direct global processes, to create an atmosphere of stability and predictability in international relations, with a firm legal basis. All nations—large and small—should be confident that their security can be reliably upheld by political means, based on international law. If this is not the case, it should come as no surprise that even the most well-intentioned states should see their only recourse in weapons buildup—and that they should choose the kinds of weapons that provide the most effective deterrent.

Russia believes in the need to involve the widest possible circle of participants in joint global efforts to secure strategic stability. The world community is vitally interested in the continued progress of the United States and Russia toward the limitation and reduction of their nuclear weapons. As early as 1999, when the issue was not as prominent on the international agenda, more than eighty member-states at the fifty-fourth UN General Assembly voted in favor of a resolution to preserve and strengthen the ABM Treaty through full and strict compliance. Even more members supported a similar resolution on the need to preserve and ensure compliance with the ABM Treaty introduced by Russia, China, and Belarus at the fifty-sixth UN General Assembly in 2001.

Washington must more fully acknowledge that the issue of strategic stability extends beyond the boundaries of Russian-American dialogue. U.S. specialists in consultation with a wide range of foreign states on antiballistic missile defense issues have corroborated this.

As various international discussions have indicated, the world is following the nuclear disarmament efforts of Russia and the United States with intense interest. For its part, Russia made significant progress in 2000: the Russian Federal Assembly ratified both START II and the Comprehensive Test Ban Treaty.

What is more encouraging is the reality that there is no reason why Russia should not continue to make further deep reductions in strategic offensive arms. This was goal was voiced explicitly by President Vladimir Putin in an official statement on November 13, 2000. In particular, President Putin suggested that both the United States and Russia should radically reduce the level of their nuclear arsenals to 1,500 warheads each. However, this is not the bottom line—Moscow is ready to consider even lower levels. Moscow also welcomed President Bush's statement that the United States intended to cut its strategic arsenal to between 1,700 and 2,200 warheads. The reductions in strategic offensive weapons proposed by Russia and announced by the United States demonstrate that good intentions by both sides in the START process produce a high level of mutual understanding. Moreover, agreements of this nature do not require protracted negotiations starting from square one. Further progress can build on the wealth of experience accumulated in our work on START I and START II, and on the contractual and legal apparatus already in place. The most important thing is a real will to move together toward radically lowering our levels of nuclear warheads. Our two countries could continue to move on parallel courses, but the drawbacks of this have been discussed above.

Russia took another significant step toward increasing strategic security in 2000 by ratifying the entire package of the New York 1997 memoranda of understanding that set clear a demarcation between strategic and nonstrategic antiballistic missile defenses.[24] The implementation of these memoranda if the United States had ratified them, would have opened up a broad area for cooperative development of nonstrategic antiballistic missile defense systems. As it stands now, the threat that this type of missile weaponry will be used is very real.

During 2001, Russia and the United States continued a detailed dialogue on antiballistic missile defense issues and the potential threat of missile technology in general. This dialogue was complicated by the two countries' serious divergence of opinion on the future of the 1972 ABM Treaty. Nevertheless, our countries continued to work together on ABM systems and theater missile defense (ABM/TMD). In fulfillment of the Joint Statement on Strategic Stability and Nuclear Security (September 1994), Russia and the United States have conducted joint ABM/TMD command and staff exercises since 1996. The most recent of these was in February 2001.

The logical extension of this type of exchange in nonstrategic missile defense was made by Vladimir Putin, who proposed in June 2000 that Russia, the United States, and NATO jointly establish a pan-European nonstrategic missile defense system. President Putin suggested several specific steps:

—jointly assess the character and scale of missile proliferation and possible missile threats

—jointly develop a concept for a pan-European system of nonstrategic ABM defense, and schedule its creation and deployment

—jointly create a pan-European early warning center

—conduct joint staff exercises, research, and experiments

—jointly develop a nonstrategic ABM defense system

—create a nonstrategic ABM defense system for joint or coordinated use to protect peacekeeping forces and civilian populations

Russia proposed that the nonstrategic ABM defense system be truly pan-European, and not restricted to a narrow bloc. This approach is superior because similar systems could subsequently be established in other regions, particularly where there are currently problems in maintaining stability and managing conflict. Thus, the Euro-ABM defense system described in structural and procedural detail and proposed to NATO and other Western partners would not need to be a one-time project. It could be seen as a pilot for regional ABM defense in general.

Another crucial focus for cooperation is the creation of a Global Monitoring System (GMS) to track missiles and missile technology proliferation. This Russian initiative has received a positive response from experts at various international meetings. GMS is not intended to replace the Missile Technology Control Regime (MTCR).[25] On the contrary, it represents an attempt to strengthen this regime by creating a link between MTCR member-states and states that remain outside this agreement.

Finally, Russia continues to welcome international efforts to bring about constructive dialogue with states about which the United States has particular concerns. Specifically, dialogue has already begun with North Korea, and steps toward reconciliation taken by North and South Korea in 2000 demonstrate that addressing international concerns through political and diplomatic means can yield significant results. Russia also made a small but valuable contribution to the Korean reconciliation: President Putin's visit to North Korea in July 2000 was a milestone in the process.

A tenable alternative to scrapping strategic stability altogether is available. What is required is a joint program of constructive efforts to ensure security, undertaken by Russia, the United States, and the entire international community. Russia firmly believes that this is a realistic goal. Moreover, we are convinced there is simply no other intelligent choice.

Admittedly, the 1990s saw significant achievements in this area. One sign of progress was the decision taken jointly by the Russian and American presidents to establish the Joint Data Exchange Center (JDEC) near Moscow in order to monitor the globe for ballistic missile launches. From Russia's point of view, representatives from the European Union, from China, and from other states could be invited to participate in the center.

We also have the opportunity today to make significant progress in stopping the spread of missile technology. Ultimately, the whole world—not just us—stands to benefit from Russian-American cooperation in nonstrategic ABM defense. Such efforts might take the form of regional systems involving all interested states that adhere to the principles of the NPT and the Comprehensive Test Ban Treaty.

Supporting strategic stability is a continuous, ongoing process that requires the world community's constant attention. Also, the concept of strategic stability itself takes on new dimensions in the modern world. As the issue of international security incorporates an ever-widening range of threats and challenges, it becomes essential to pursue global strategic stability as a comprehensive way to work toward the creation of a twenty-first-century democratic world order. In other words, strategic stability must be viewed in the widest possible sense of the phrase.

This is the approach Russia took at the 2000 United Nations Millennium Assembly and its summit. There, the Russian delegation proposed a detailed concept for strategic stability containing specific ways to address today's most pressing issues. The proposal called primarily for further progress in disarmament and more effective barriers to the spread of weapons of mass destruction. In this day and age, the issues of nuclear nonproliferation and disarmament no longer involve only Russia, the United States, and other nuclear powers. The multilateral mechanisms of the UN and the world community must be brought to bear on these processes. This will require consistent joint efforts to adhere strictly to agreements already in effect. It will require the gradual reduction, and ultimately the elimination, of weapons of mass destruction, accompanied by effective international monitoring and limitation of other kinds of weapons. And it will require that we not allow arms races to begin in any new areas.

Russia has made a series of specific proposals on key international issues relating to disarmament. These include jump-starting the Conference on Disarmament, putting adoption of the CTBT on a fast track, and further strengthening the NPT. At the Millennium Summit, President Putin proposed an initiative to develop and carry out an international project under the aegis of the International Atomic Energy Agency (IAEA) to gradually phase out the use of enriched uranium and separated plutonium as fuel sources by the nuclear power industry. And in November 2000 President Putin made broad new proposals for strengthening strategic stability and further reducing nuclear arsenals.

Russia believes that strategic stability means strengthening peace and security on all continents. It also means effectively managing existing regional conflicts, while preventing new ones. This can be achieved only through the joint efforts of all nations, who are collectively responsible for the future of our world. Experience has shown that unilateral use of force cannot bring about a long-lasting and fair solution to crisis.

Strategic stability also means maintaining reliable international information security and counteracting misuse of the technological revolution to harm our overall progress and undermine the international community. Recognizing the importance of these issues, Russia initiated a UN examination of "developments in the field of information and telecommunications technology in the context of international information security."

Strategic stability means a guarantee of peace and security for both civilian society and the individual. This can be attained only through the world community's unified efforts to counter the threats and challenges we face today, in particular, aggressive separatism and religious extremism, and the illegal arms trade and organized crime.

Already mentioned above is the direct threat that the extremist aberration of international terrorism poses to security and stability. Unfortunately, recent events have convincingly demonstrated that terrorists of all stripes have the ability to work more effectively than the world community that opposes them. Russia believes that international cooperation in the fight against terrorism should be based on the principles clearly established by the UN Security Council's resolution 1269: that no state should support or give safe haven to terrorists, and that no terrorist act must go unpunished. The UN Security Council should take action against those who violate these principles, in accordance with the UN Charter. Russia intends to ratify the UN's Convention on Financial Terrorism and considers it imperative to finalize a convention against acts of nuclear terrorism and to continue to work toward a comprehensive convention against all forms of terrorism. Because terrorism is often closely connected with the drug trade and organized crime, our country has also supported an international convention against organized crime. An international convention against corruption would also have significant merit.

Strategic stability means universal freedom and rights for the individual. This figures prominently in the efforts of international organizations as they establish a new world order based on standards of law. Russia is making a sizable contribution toward efforts to establish a universal legal code. We are a signatory to the Rome Statute of the International Criminal Court. We are also a party to the optional protocols to the Convention on the Rights of the Child and to the Optional Protocol to the Convention on the Elimination of all Forms of Discrimination against Women.

Still, for all the progress that has been made in the half century since the fascist defeat in World War II, the world continues to suffer complications from pockets of xenophobia, militant nationalism, and ethnic and religious intolerance. We cannot continue to sit idly by as many countries (Latvia, for example) forbid groups of people to speak their native languages, or deny them citizenship or employment based on ethnicity. It is impermissible that former fascists are treated favorably by the authorities, yet those who fight against fascism are imprisoned. The UN, the Council of Europe, the Organization for Security and Cooperation in Europe (OSCE), and other international organizations cannot be complacent in the face of these phenomena. We must respond decisively, with no double standards.

Strategic stability needs to have a strong material base. It is possible that our century will be remembered as that in which mankind made a quantum developmental leap forward. But this will be true only if the peace and international security we achieve is accompanied by a more dynamic and aggressive process of economic and technological equalization between the huge bulk of developing states and the relatively small group of leading states. Clearly, this is a long-term problem. It requires that we establish—guided and coordinated by the UN—a means to manage collectively and democratically the systems of international finance, trade, and economics. These systems need to be rationalized and made more equitable, and to do more to help fight poverty and underdevelopment.

We must make maximum use of new opportunities made possible by the technological revolution to start reducing the divide between the rich and the poor, rather than allowing the gap to continue to widen. This process could be driven by new information and communications technology, which has the same potential for accelerating global progress as the invention of writing had. We have the chance to skip several traditional developmental stages because of the worldwide spread of information technology and computer literacy. Armed with these powerful tools, mankind truly has the chance to create the conditions for each individual on earth to achieve his or her full potential and live the life he or she deserves. We must use this chance wisely and effectively.

Strategic stability means preserving a clean and healthy environment for this and future generations. The UN has done much to mobilize international efforts on this vital front. Russia supports the cultivation of international cooperation in areas such as biodiversity, climate, the fight against desertification, and forest preservation.

The increase in recent years of natural and man-made ecological disasters, and the increasing rate of death and property loss from them, makes disaster prevention and mitigation one of the most challenging problems facing mankind today. As the UN works to develop international cooperation in this area, we must be sure to identify the most modern and specialized technology available for this purpose, and to use it in the most innovative ways.

Thus, Russia understands the idea of "strategic stability" as a conceptual basis uniting the international community's efforts to resolve the most pressing global issues, and in the future to establish the democratic world order mankind needs to develop and prosper.

Russia and the United Nations

A primary element to be found in the Russian Foreign Policy Concept is support for strengthening the UN as an overarching instrument for attaining international peace and security. As far as Russia's national interests are concerned, the significance of our policies in the framework of a global organization is determined by two fundamental circumstances. First, the Russian Federation is a permanent member of the UN Security Council, which carries some measure of responsibility to support peace efforts. Second, the UN has an indispensable role as the organizational structure for establishing a democratic, multipolar system of international relations.

Russia was present at the creation of the United Nations, one of the twentieth century's most significant events. The UN brought to life one of mankind's oldest ideas—that there should exist a universal, global organization whose mission would be to unify the nations of the world into a community without war, where law and fairness should prevail. As any entity that goes beyond mere speculative design to actually attempt effective solutions to specific real-life problems, the UN has made its share of mistakes and has had its share of failures. On balance, however, the world body has entered the new century in an unquestionably positive light.

Although the world has not evolved into the ideal we would like since the UN's formation, and armed conflicts continue to flare up in various regions, the UN's historic accomplishment is that it has helped mankind avoid a third world war, which would undoubtedly have been civilization's last. Despite the radical reconfiguration of the global balance of power that existed in 1945, the UN continues to prove its viability. For half a century, its charter has served as the central document for international law and the basis for civilized contact between states. UN secretary-general Kofi Annan was right when he stated that the "relevance and capacity of the United Nations' purposes and principles to inspire have in no way diminished. If anything they have increased."[26] Everyone today acknowledges that without the UN and its charter's principles of nonaggression, sovereignty, self-determination, equal rights, and respect for individual rights and freedoms, the world would be a much more dangerous and unstable place.

The UN's most significant achievement was to establish a formal means whereby states could reach compatible positions to collectively settle their international disputes. The United Nations is responsible for weaving a culture of multilateral dialogue into the fabric of international relations. Without this, modern international life would be unthinkable. The myriad regional, subregional, and other organizations that have been formed have not diminished the UN's role in the least. On the contrary, these organizations all strive to interact with the UN in some way or other. By working with these regional partners, the UN is able to channel their efforts into achieving the goals set forth in its charter.

Consistently striving to motivate states to use peaceful means of dispute settlement, the UN created the theory and practice of peace making, peacekeeping and peace building. The UN continues to develop this body of knowledge and experience in light of the new realities that have

come into force with the end of the cold war—that the majority of conflicts around the world have nothing to do with intergovernmental disagreement, but are entirely internal in nature.

In his "Report on the Work of the Organization" from the forty-ninth
session to the fiftieth session, former UN secretary-general Boutros
Boutros-Ghali noted that

> the opinion was widespread that the many regional conflicts that
> had flared up in various parts of the world could be quickly extin-
> guished. . . . Sadly, these optimistic hopes have been largely dashed
> by world events in the past several years. Many old conflicts con-
> tinue unabated despite the world community's efforts to manage
> them. The outbreak of new wars continues, with nearly all being
> intra-national."[27]

These words, spoken in the mid-1990s, are still accurate today. The
developmental disparity between a relatively small group of states and
entire regions has led to a situation where the freedoms enjoyed by some
come at a burdensome cost to others. Therefore, attaining fair and equitable global balance must retain a prominent place on the UN's agenda
into the future.

The UN's reputation as a just and unbiased arbiter is evidenced by the
fact that parties in conflict generally seek mediation from the organization, counting on its peace-making ability. Since the UN's inception, there
have been fifty-five Peace Support Operations (PSO), of which forty-two
were sanctioned from 1988 to 2000. It is no exaggeration to describe many
of these as historic efforts. A UN peace support operation stopped the
collapse of the Congo in the 1960s, and and others were determining factors in regulating conflicts in Mozambique, Namibia, Kampuchea,
El Salvador, Nicaragua, Guatemala, and Tajikistan. In most of the fifteen
PSOs currently in effect, the operation's deployment was accompanied by
the UN's active political involvement in regulating the conflicts in these
regions. An extremely successful example of this type of effort was in
Tajikistan, where the UN and the CIS played active roles in regulating the
internal conflict and achieving a full agreement on national peace.

In their charter, the UN founding fathers provided for the use of
regional organizations for peacekeeping purposes. They did so, however,
clearly stipulating that the Security Council must sanction the use of

force or other elements of compulsion. The foresight of the charter's authors has been proved in practice more than once. Attempts to circumvent this basic requirement of the charter and use unilateral force have not ended well. An objective observer will see this in the profound protracted crisis in Iraq, and in the explosive situation in and around the Yugoslav region of Kosovo.

It is becoming more widely acknowledged that trying to resolve matters of war and peace without involving the UN has little hope of success. Until recently, for example, some expressed doubt about the need to actively involve the UN in the Middle East peace process. Now, however, it is generally accepted that the UN plays a key role in achieving stability on the Lebanese-Israeli border after the withdrawal of Israeli troops from southern Lebanon.

The UN is firmly established as the primary forum for multilateral disarmament issues. The UN mobilizes political support for the nonproliferation of weapons of mass destruction and provides enormous encouragement and stimulus to parties engaged in bilateral talks on strategic offensive weapons reduction. The November 2001 General Assembly resolution on the preservation of and compliance with the 1972 ABM Treaty is extremely important in this regard.[28] The UN is directly involved in putting a stop to the illicit trafficking in small arms and light weapons that play such a central role in the outbreak and fueling of interethnic conflict and terrorism.

The UN must not simply accumulate the positive baggage of its international peace process successes, it must also learn from its negative experiences. This is particularly true in its use of sanctions against those who violate international law. Since the 1970s—when the world community's strict sanctions against South Africa and Rhodesia resulted in the overthrow of apartheid—it is difficult to identify any instance where a just cause has been achieved with this tool. Overzealous and indiscriminate use of comprehensive, open-ended sanctions in the early 1990s (of the fifteen cases of regimes being sanctioned in the UN's entire history, thirteen have occurred since 1991) has resulted in the suffering of the populace in the countries against which sanctions were in effect and in neighboring states. The effect of sanctions on people's lives, on the economy, and on the future of civil society in general has been especially harsh in Iraq.

Today the international community is engaged in a conceptual debate over how best to shift away from the discredited use of indiscriminate sanctions toward other means of exerting influence directly on specific individuals who violate international law and sabotage the Security Council's resolutions. For example, calibrated, targeted sanctions were put in place against the Taliban in Afghanistan to make them stop supporting international terrorism (after large-scale aid from the Taliban to Chechen rebels had been confirmed). In addition, Russia and other similarly minded states are trying to get the Security Council to stop setting up sanctions regimes that are open-ended. Instead, sanctions should expire after a set period, their possible humanitarian consequences should be analyzed, measures should be taken to spare the civilian population from suffering, and neighboring countries should not be affected. As a result, the UN General Assembly—which had already supported this approach for the Security Council's use of sanctions regimes—is implementing resolutions in this area. This new view on the use of sanctions is reflected in the aspirations of the nonaligned states. The outcome of the April 2000 Ministerial Conference of the Non-Aligned Countries held in Cartageña emphasized that sanctions should be imposed for a specified time-frame and be based on tenable legal grounds, and that they should not be applied to achieve political ends.[29]

The UN coordinates the world's efforts to counter new threats and meet new challenges by providing a much-needed international legal base. Under the supervision of the UN, new conventions on the war against terrorism and its financing have been adopted and several significant conventions on the illegal drug trade have been concluded. The Convention against Transnational Organized Crime—adopted during the General Assembly's fifty-fifth session and signed at the 2000 Palermo Conference—signified the start of a new stage in international cooperative efforts aimed at fighting crime.

Generally, the UN has become the international authority for establishing multilateral standards. More international legal instruments have been produced during the period of the UN's existence than had been produced during the entire history of the world up to that point.

The UN carries out significant social and economic work. The system of UN offices is made up of the General Assembly, the Economic and

Security Councils and their committees and commissions, fourteen specialized entities, and various programs and funds. These bodies encompass cooperative national efforts in all areas of modern life: economics and finance, agriculture, health, labor relations, science and culture, intellectual property, meteorology, air and sea transportation, telecommunications, and mail delivery, and so forth.

Although the UN itself has few financial resources to carry out development projects around the world, it plays an increasingly central role in the reform of the world's financial system. A series of UN World Conferences during the 1990s on the environment, human rights, population, development, women, and urban development have established a conceptual basis for the collective creation of an economic world order that should no longer ignore our most burning social and economic issues. The UN's persistence in addressing these issues has induced the key multilateral financial institutions—the International Monetary Fund and the World Bank group—to make poverty, health, aid to the poorest countries, and social aspects of market reform high priorities. Today, the UN essentially adds a sociological dimension to global economic and financial politics and facilitates international democratization. It was in the UN that the concept of sustainable development comprising the gamut of economic, social, and environmental issues was developed and gained universal recognition.

The UN has also led efforts to address the issue of refugees. According to statistics from the Office of the UN High Commissioner for Refugees (UNHCR), these efforts have resulted in a gradual reduction in the number of refugees worldwide: from 17.6 million in 1992 to 13.6 million in 1997,[30] down to an estimated 11.5 million in 1999. The largely internal nature of most of today's conflicts leads less to the production of refugees than it does to internally displaced persons (IDPs). The UN is reorganizing somewhat so as to more effectively address, with the blessing of the sovereign states involved, the issue of IDPs, who number 25 million individuals worldwide.[31]

The UN was the first body to recognize the states with so-called transitional economies as a group. The UN passed a series of important resolutions on the need to support the efforts of these countries, including Russia, to implement social and economic reforms and to integrate, when possible, into the global economic and trade system. Based on these resolutions, Russia receives resources from various UN programs and funds to carry out specific projects supporting its reforms and social programs, primarily at the regional level.

The aforementioned list of UN accomplishments, each of which is in Russia's national interest, should convince the reader how importantly the organization figures in Russia's foreign policy. As a universal forum, the UN fulfills a vital monitoring function to ensure that no one government or organization steps outside the bounds of international law. All international and regional structures, without exception, are represented at the UN. Their common language creates the optimal environment for finding balanced and broadly acceptable—and therefore realizable—approaches to world affairs.

The UN system forms a natural center for uniting the efforts of all member-states. It is their political will that determines the future of the United Nations' authority. Russia sees the UN's changes as a set of measures that will heighten the organization's international role. Keeping in mind the accelerating rate of change we face today, Secretary-General Kofi Annan has correctly observed that the UN's reforms are not a one-time event but a process, one that ensures that the organization keeps abreast of real-life events.

At their current stage, the reforms emphasize many goals. These are, primarily, developing reliable ways of avoiding crisis, increasing the effectiveness of peace making and strengthening its basis in close interaction with regional organizations and with a central charter role played by the Security Council, assisting in multilateral disarmament and in efforts toward the nonproliferation of weapons of mass destruction, fighting international terrorism and organized crime, stepping up measures to eliminate poverty and protect the environment, settling the refugee issue, and bringing some order to the process of immigration.

The Security Council is part and parcel of these reforms. It must become more representative, yet retain its effectiveness and ability to act swiftly. It is unproductive to paint a picture that faults the Security Council for not developing a unified approach in favor of sanctions against the use of force, to stop humanitarian disaster. Certain countries or organizations (NATO, for instance), perceive that this lack of clear prohibition gives them free rein to "punish those who cause civilian suffering" and to "restore justice" as they see fit.

In cases like these, the Security Council is fettered by the power of veto held by its member-states. It is important to remember the following. First, the right to veto is based on the principle of the UN Charter that requires unanimity among all of the Security Council's five permanent members. This is not merely a privilege, but rather, a key principle of post-World War II international relations created to guarantee that no international actions would take place that went against the national interests of any of the great powers. The vitality of the UN lies in this key principle. It is this principle that has the potential to form a multipolar world, which is the only way to maintain a stable and reliable world order.

This does not mean that the Security Council's permanent members are free to use the veto whenever they feel like it. On the contrary, as the interdependence of all nations grows and international cooperation expands, and as democratization spreads across the globe, the Security Council—and the "big five," in particular—will be much more strongly influenced by the rest of the world's nations. Today, the Security Council does not pass a single resolution, especially involving measures of compulsion, without considering as carefully as possible the views of all interested UN members. Present circumstances make it practically impossible to veto an item without a crystal-clear explanation of the reason. Similarly, it is extremely difficult to use the power of the veto to pursue an illegal goal or to block a resolution that represents an honorable attempt by the world community to stop gross or widespread human rights violations.

Russia takes its current responsibilities as a permanent member of the Security Council very seriously. We also actively seek to increase the council's capability to respond effectively to humanitarian crisis. Russia introduced a UN initiative to clarify the legal aspects of the collective use of force as a foreign relations tool in the context of today's globalized world. The UN must also devote serious study to further developing specific methods of preventive diplomacy and peace making, to improving the efficiency of sanctions regimes, and to improving the methodology and practice of postconflict peace building.

The UN's founding fathers anticipated the need to respond—legally—to breaches of peace and security.[32] The world community can resort to measures of compulsion, but only in accordance with the UN Charter and by decision of the Security Council, for illegal means only serve to compromise legal goals. Measures of compulsion must be used with exceptional care and must not be used as repressive instruments to influence a particular nation or people that has attracted the disfavor of someone else.

The evolution of peace processes dictates the suitability of new international legal standards and their adaptation to new realities. However, these advances must be made through collective discussion and decisionmaking. Such efforts cannot be started from scratch; they must be based on existing standards of international law.

On the whole, given the willingness of all states, and based on the UN Charter and on the wealth of experience it represents, it is both necessary and possible to conduct sensible reforms that strengthen the UN's role in the world. Within the organization's charter are contained all the resources necessary to formulate creditable, global responses to the global challenges we face today. But we can only unleash this potential effectively together, without individual claims for unconditional leadership and without trying to impose an individual worldview. Our future lies in the UN's ability to join new ideas and trends in development with tried and true principles of international law and order.

Announcing the first Bush-Putin meeting with Colin Powell in Washington, May 19, 2001.

3

REGIONAL TRENDS IN
RUSSIAN FOREIGN POLICY

The Commonwealth of Independent States

From the very first day of its existence, the most crucial foreign policy issue for the new Russia has been its relationship with the Commonwealth of Independent States. The collapse of the USSR led to unprecedented changes across an enormous geopolitical space, populated by dozens of diverse ethnic groups. These changes have directly, and often dramatically, affected the lives of millions of our compatriots. This is why the problem of creating a new system of international relations in the space of the former USSR continues to be one of the highest foreign policy priorities for the Russian leadership. Over the past decade, however, Russia has frequently made corrections both to its vision of the CIS and to its actual policy initiatives toward the other members of the Commonwealth.

During the Commonwealth's early stages, many felt that the historical ties that had developed between the Soviet republics and forged them into a single political and economic organism would be a sufficient precondition for the CIS to quickly evolve into a full-fledged, integrated union of states. This view left a strong mark in the Commonwealth's founding documents. When they signed the Agreement on the Establishment of the Commonwealth of Independent States, the member-states announced their intentions to preserve and maintain a common space—socioeconomic, military and strategic, and in transportation—on the territory of the former USSR.[1] Short-term goals set forth by the member-states of the CIS included keeping the internal, republican borders porous by focusing upon the collective defense of the external border of the CIS; coordinating foreign policies; creating a mechanism to ensure the payment of social security and retirement benefits for veterans and their families; guaranteeing every citizen of the CIS equal rights and liberties in accordance with accepted international standards, regardless of nationality and country of domicile; and continuing formal exchanges of information, of culture, and so on, among the member-states.

Nevertheless, the real politics of CIS members immediately began to diverge farther and farther from these goals. Centrifugal forces in politics, trade, and economics made it increasingly difficult to create and sustain active mutually beneficial cooperation. In many ways, this evolution was an objective process. The economic ties between former Soviet republics were based on a command economy that primarily functioned because of extreme centralization and Communist Party control. Toward the end of the 1980s, the system was already beginning to come apart at the seams. When the government holding it together collapsed and the transition to a market economy began, the old system simply ceased to exist. This was bound to result in a serious crisis for the entire structure of post-Soviet economic interaction. Market reforms in Russia and the other Commonwealth states varied widely in their content and in the speed with which they were carried out, which did nothing to help bring the member-states closer economically. And finally, some of the states shifted their policies, to reorient their trade and economic ties away from the CIS and toward other regions of the world.

All of this led to a significant decrease in the volume of trade within the CIS. In 1991, trade between CIS member states accounted for 60 percent of the CIS volume of trade. That figure had been halved by 1999. From 1988 to 1990, trade between republics within the borders of the former Soviet Union accounted for one-quarter of gross domestic product; now the figure is 10 percent. And during this same period, the share of Russia's foreign trade that went to CIS member-states declined by approximately 22 percent.

In light of substantial policy differences between CIS member-states, the CIS Economic Union posited in the September 24, 1993, agreement has never been realized. The Payments and Currency Unions never came into being. In general, this early stage was characterized by growing disparity between the political statements and official agreements that seemed to further the Commonwealth's development and the degree to which they were implemented in the real world. For example, from 1991 to 1998, 1,030 multilateral international agreements and treaties were signed within the CIS. However, many of them exist only on paper. Of the 164 documents adopted by the Council of Heads of State (CIS-CHS) and the Council of Heads of Governments (CIS-CHG) that were to ratify or implement intrastate procedures, only seven have gone into effect for all signatory states (on February 1, 2000).[2]

The centrifugal forces had their effect on politics as well. Differences emerged in member-states' views on the Commonwealth's fundamental goals and purpose and on its role in international affairs. In many ways, this was due to the psychological difficulties experienced by the CIS states as they adjusted to an entirely new way of relating to each other. These difficulties were most strongly felt by the newly independent states that at first had neither the experience nor the qualified personnel needed to sustain an independent foreign policy. Before acting or being treated as new actors in the international arena, these states had to go through the process of crafting a national identity for themselves. In some cases, this was accomplished at the cost of weakened ties to Russia. Moreover, logistically, a certain amount of time was needed to bring relations between Russia and its CIS partners into a pattern of diplomacy normal for the rest of the world.

Still, it would be a mistake to see only the negative aspects of the Commonwealth's early stage. The historic significance of that period is that cooperation within the CIS, for all its failings and imperfections, stopped the former Soviet Union from descending into chaos. It is obvious what the consequences would have been had events taken a turn toward balkanization, especially given the large stockpiles of weapons of mass destruction housed throughout the territory of the former Soviet Union. Under the circumstances, the agreement on the dismantling of nuclear weapons held by Ukraine, Belarus, and Kazakhstan was a historic achievement of diplomacy between Russia and its Commonwealth partners. The agreement provided a reliable guarantee of security in the former USSR.

In September 1995, President Yeltsin issued a decree on the Establishment of the Strategic Course of Russia with Member States of the Commonwealth of Independent States (CIS).[3] This document affirmed the priority of this direction in Russia's foreign policy. The Strategic Course proceeded from the fact that the situation in the former Soviet Union was vitally important to Russia's economy, defense, and security, and to the rights of Russian citizens outside Russia. Clearly, consolidation efforts were needed.

Russia identified four main goals vis-à-vis the other CIS states: to ensure reliable stability in all areas—politics, the military, economics, humanitarian concerns, and law enforcement; to help transform CIS countries into politically and economically stable states, with policies friendly to Russia; to strengthen Russia's leadership role in the creation of a new system of intergovernmental political and economic relations; and to extend and further institutionalize the process of integration among the member-states of the CIS.

The founding documents of Russia's CIS policy, produced in the mid-1990s, were aimed at preserving the former Soviet Union's geopolitical space as a "special interest zone" for Russia. Moreover, Russia was now committed to pursuing policies that would deepen integration among members of the CIS and transform the Commonwealth into an influential entity in world politics and economics. It was only natural that the leadership and organizational role for this effort after the Soviet collapse fell to Russia. Russia's main policy goal for the CIS was to create an economically and politically integrated union of states capable of claiming a worthy place in the world.

However, by the mid-1990s it gradually became expedient for Russia to bring its CIS policies into line with a more realistic evaluation of the Commonwealth's future. Russia's approach to the CIS eventually made it possible to pursue a "two-track" strategy toward CIS integration. On one hand, there existed a more-or-less integrated nucleus of states prepared to move to a higher level of cooperation. This group was followed, on the other hand, by the remaining states that would join as they were able.

This two-tier development reflected the gradual process of political and economic stratification that had taken place in the CIS since the first half of the 1990s. This stratification is what turned the two-track integration model into a reality.

The epitome of integration within the CIS was set by the course of Russia-Belarus relations. On April 2, 1996, these two countries signed the Treaty on the Establishment of a Community of Belarus and Russia, followed exactly one year later by an augmented Treaty on Union between Belarus and Russia, and finally, by the Union Treaty signed on December 8, 1999.[4] Efforts have been under way to fully realize the treaty's provisions. Administrative offices for the new union government were created, and joint institutions were established to coordinate policy, including foreign policy. Soon, it became a priority to put some real meat on the bones of the union, especially in economics. There is no doubt that success in this endeavor will be a powerful catalyst for integration across the Commonwealth.

On March 29, 1996, a four-state accord, the Treaty on Deepening Integration in Economic and Humanitarian Spheres, was signed March 29, 1996, by Belarus, Kazakhstan, Kyrgyzstan, and Russia.[5] Tajikistan acceded to this treaty as the fifth member of this group in 1999. These states undertook joint efforts to further integration with the creation of a Customs Union, which in October 2000 was transformed into a full-fledged international economic organization: the Eurasian Economic Union (EEU). These five countries plus Armenia also pursue joint military and political cooperation as signatories of a collective security agreement. Other attempts at greater integration include the decision by Kazakhstan, Kyrgyzstan, Uzbekistan, and Tajikistan to join forces to create the Central Asian Economic Union (CAEU), an organization in which Russia holds observer status. Georgia, Ukraine, Uzbekistan, Azerbaijan, and Moldova have also undertaken efforts to promote closer relations via the creation of the GUUAM union. Turkmenistan, however, occupies a unique position within the CIS, having proclaimed itself a neutral state. The government regularly abstains from signing resolutions that are adopted by CIS bodies, even with the participation of Turkmen leadership.

At the same time, all CIS states expressed interest in creating a free trade zone. Initiated by Russia, four agreements were signed: a treaty on coordinated antimonopoly policy, an agreement on common licensing procedures and customs controls for goods transported between CIS member-states, a protocol on procedure for consultation on gradual withdrawal from free trade, and an agreement on technical barriers in the free trade zone.

The dawn of the twenty-first century brings with it a new stage in Russian policy toward the CIS. The point of departure for rethinking Russian policy was recognition of the need for more realistic evaluation of the viability of the Commonwealth's transformation into an integrated supranational entity. Essentially, Russia was faced with a dilemma. Should we continue to hold integration as an absolute value, for which we would pay any price and make any concessions to our partners? Or should we take a more pragmatic tack, making sure our fundamental national interests of security and economic development were met, even at the price of deepening CIS integration?

In the final analysis, Russia chose to deepen bilateral ties with other CIS member-states as a prerequisite for further integration. Relations with each of these CIS states are presently formulated according to their level of reciprocal interest in cooperation and their willingness to take Russia's interests into account, particularly with respect to security and to the rights of Russian nationals living within their borders. This pragmatic approach has already begun to yield positive results; Russia is developing balanced and mutually respectful relations with the majority of CIS states.

During 2000–01 Russia was able to enter into serious multidimensional dialogue with Ukraine, including at the highest level. We have made progress toward resolving many thorny bilateral issues, especially those having to do with economics, such as nonpayment of debt and the trade imbalance. The trend has been for our positions to converge on many key international issues.

Russia also became more active in Central Asia during this period, focusing much attention on strengthening cooperation in security, especially joint efforts to counteract the international terrorist threat. For the first time in recent years, we were able to turn around the decline of our trade volume in Central Asia and to bring about a substantial increase.

Intense dialogue at the highest level has advanced our relations with Azerbaijan. Our cooperation with Armenia functions on the level of allies. On the other hand, relations with Georgia have been problematic. Russia is prepared to normalize relations with Tbilisi if consideration is given to our interests, especially with regard to international terrorism.

Russia views bilateral relations with other CIS states as an essential step in the deepening of our mutual multilateral efforts toward integration. We have always expressed our willingness in this regard. However, integration is not a goal in and of itself. Our integration must be organic, as a natural response to problems that logically call for, and sometimes demand, a joint solution. The world's experience with integration shows that the process cannot be artificially forced, but has a whole set of economic and political objective prerequisites. For example, the first integrated unions in Latin America were formed in the 1960s. Yet it took three decades before their success really became evident.

The experience of every integrated union in the world also shows that a high degree of mutual political understanding and trust among the member-states is required for success. It is not surprising, for example, that the United States plays a central role in NAFTA or that the German economy is central to the EU. Thus, it is natural to suppose a pivotal role for Russia in the CIS by virtue of its size, its population, and its economic capability.

Russia seeks neither to force integration on any of the CIS states nor to exclude any that are truly interested. We also feel it is normal for CIS states to diversify their international ties and to seek out new trade and economic partners. However, Russia will not tolerate attempts by third-party states to act within the CIS in a way that undermines Russian interests, excludes Russia from participating, or in any way weakens Russia's position. This kind of competition and fight for "spheres of influence" is clearly an anachronism in world politics and serves only to taint international relations with tension and mistrust.

Although the interests of CIS member states vary widely, all the members share an objective interest in mutually beneficial cooperation in several specific areas. The majority of them are prepared to seek joint responses to today's new threats and challenges of terrorism, militant separatism and religious extremism, transnational crime, and the illegal drug trade.

On June 21, 2000, in Moscow, the Council of CIS Heads of State adopted the program for combating international terrorism and extremism for the period to 2003. They also adopted a resolution to establish the CIS Anti-Terrorism Center in Moscow, which has the Russian Federal Security Service (FSB) at its core. The CIS Summit in Moscow was notable for an important act that signified a breakthrough in the member-states' political interaction. For the first time ever, the presidents examined—at Russia's initiation—the enormous issue of setting global peace policy and agreed on a final document. The world's positive reaction to the Statement of the CIS Heads of State Supporting Strategic Stability—which confirmed the immutable significance of the 1972 ABM Treaty and emphasized the danger posed by attempts to undermine it—in turn helped to increase the credibility of the CIS in the eyes of the world.

Today, the primary instrument consolidating CIS joint security efforts and for promoting military-technical cooperation is the Collective Security Treaty (CST).[6] This treaty was extended for another five-year period in 1999. In May 2000, the Collective Security Council approved a package of documents adapting the CST to new geopolitical realities and significantly expanding and strengthening portions of the treaty. The revamped treaty was further secured by activities and programs carried out by the council and its groups in 2001.

Russia champions multilateral cooperation in many other areas: foreign policy, culture, education, health, and information exchange. A detailed plan of action (to 2005) has been worked out to realize the main goals set by the CIS Heads of State in their April 2, 1999, declaration.

The CIS is presently undergoing a process of belt tightening, normal for any regional union of states. In lieu of original ambitious plans to create a deeply integrated Economic Union, the CIS has begun to focus on structural reforms. In 1999, Russia stopped pushing for the Commonwealth's institutions and agencies to be given national authority, to which the majority of members-states had objected.

Thematic efforts to reform the CIS organizational structure have been ongoing since April 1999. The Executive Committee was established as a single permanent body responsible for executive functions, administration, and coordination. The Economic Council was established to implement decisions made by CIS leadership regarding the creation and operation of a free trade zone, and other issues of social and economic cooperation.

The CIS faces a major problem in the regulation of conflict within its borders, in Abkhazia, South Ossetia, Nagorno-Karabakh, and the Trans-Dniester (Moldova). Efforts by Russia in conjunction with the UN and OSCE in each of these post-Soviet hot spots have produced the cessation of military action, permanent cease-fires, and the conditions needed for political conflict resolution to begin. The goal at this stage is to prevent violence from breaking out again, and to help the combatants reach mutually acceptable peaceful resolutions.

Contingents of Russian peace-making forces were deployed by virtue of bilateral agreements and CIS-CHS resolutions to Abkhazia, South Ossetia, and Trans-Dniester. For many reasons, Russia has ended up playing this role of peacekeeper virtually alone. Despite attempts by some in the West to disparage the efforts of our peacekeeping troops, their decisive contribution to the stabilization of these hot spots in the CIS has won wide recognition by the international community.

A great peacekeeping achievement in recent years was the successful regulation—with Russia's decisive contribution—of the Tajik civil war, which allowed nearly one million refugees to return to their homeland. The newly elected parliament—the Majlis Oli—began operation at the end of March 2000 in Dushanbe, and the Commission on National Reconciliation announced that it was disbanding, having fulfilled its objective. Still, there remains much to do before life in Tajikistan returns to normal. It will be a long process. As long as neighboring Afghanistan remains unsettled, long-term stability in Tajikistan remains in jeopardy. Russia consistently seeks wider international support for the transformation of Tajikistan, for instance, in opening a postconflict UN peacekeeping office in Dushanbe, and in calling an international conference or roundtable of donors who could mobilize foreign financial aid for this country.

The prolonged limbo of neither war nor peace in the Caucasus region directly bordering Russia is of vital concern to us. The situation in the Caucasus is directly tied to the Azerbaijan-Armenian standoff on the issue of Nagorno-Karabakh. This conflict continues to disrupt trade and economic exchange between these two countries and Russia, it prevents full-fledged multilateral interaction in the Caucasus, and it creates tension at the southern edge of our country. The key to bringing peace to the region is held by the two states themselves, which bear primary responsibility for finding a solution to the difficult issue of Karabakh. The eventual resolution must create peace in the region with neither victor nor vanquished, and must make permanent stability possible in the region. It is essential that Baku and Yerevan come to the resolution of their conflict in good faith.

In the midst of this complex situation, Russian diplomacy operates both independently and together with international intermediaries to focus on keeping the direct negotiation process open between Azerbaijan and Armenia, right up to the highest level. Russia is willing to accept any plan that regulates this conflict in a manner acceptable to both sides and that could serve to guarantee that an agreement of compromise could be worked out.

Guided by this approach, Russia facilitated the resurrection of Azerbaijan-Armenian political dialogue at the highest level. At each of the successive meetings initiated by Russia, the leaders of these two countries were able gradually to develop the levels of trust needed to start the process of building peace in their region. There have been prisoner exchanges, cease-fires have become more regular and reliable, and the two countries' military and foreign policy agencies are maintaining regular contact.

There is no doubt that fair, stable, and peaceful regulation of the Nagorno-Karabakh conflict will go far to help the joint efforts of Azerbaijan, Armenia, Georgia, and Russia to transform the Caucasus into a peaceful, open, and prosperous region. In the meantime, the "Caucasus Four" has come into its own in recent years, working at full steam. The regular Caucasus Four summit meetings are creating the political environment needed for constructive political solutions to emerge.

Unfortunately, the intractable standoff in the Georgia-Abkhazia conflict has long impeded any constructive search for compromise. The main unresolved issues here are the final political status of Abkhazia and the return of refugees. The central challenge is to construct a peaceful arrangement that will respect Georgia's territorial integrity, yet is acceptable to the Abkhazians.

The focus of our approach to regulation of the Trans-Dniester conflict is simple: we are working actively to reach a political resolution that is in the interests of the tens of thousands of Moldovans, Russians, Ukrainians, and indeed any group that has settled on the banks of the Dniester. We feel this is an attainable goal and that the formula for regulation must include two elements: to preserve the territorial integrity of Moldova within its 1990 borders and to grant Trans-Dniester a measure of territorial and governmental autonomy within the Republic of Moldova. The success of efforts to regulate the conflict in this area is directly tied to the presence in the Trans-Dniester of stockpiles of arms and ammunition belonging to Russian troops and accumulated over decades. These arms and ammunition are being transported out of the region, in conjunction with Russia's obligations under the Conventional Forces in Europe (CFE) Treaty. Russia will continue to address this problem in light of the conditions accepted at the November 1999 OSCE summit in Istanbul.[7]

The last decade has clearly shown both how complicated the integration process in the CIS is and what great promise it holds. Russia is guided by the firm conviction that the CIS has the capability to become an influential regional organization that stimulates prosperity, cooperation, and openness within the space of the former Soviet Union. Kasymzhomart K. Tokaev, former prime minister of the Republic of Kazakhstan, expressed the situation succinctly when he said, "the economic crisis experienced by all post-Soviet states makes their coordinated efforts, constructive cooperation, and search for mutually acceptable solutions absolutely essential. Without this, it will be impossible to maintain stability, ensure security, reform our economies, or to integrate with the world community."[8]

Still, the ten-year history of the CIS tells us we must be realistic. The glue that holds the Commonwealth together for the foreseeable future must be good-neighborly, mutually beneficial, bilateral relations between all member-states.

Since their approval by President Putin, Russia's new principles for CIS policy have produced positive changes in the relationships between Russia and her partners. Firmly committed to recognizing mutual interests, CIS policy has become more pragmatic, more transparent, and more predictable. In addition, there has been welcome development on the trade and economics front: the 2000 volume of trade between Russia and CIS member-states increased more than 40 percent from the previous year, exceeding $25 billion.

This stage in the Commonwealth's evolution brings us not only new opportunities, but new problems as well. Primarily, we will need to make more of an effort to strike the optimal balance between multilateral and bilateral forms of interaction, between economic and political goals in decisionmaking, and between short-term and long-term goals.

Europe

The interrelationship of Russia and Europe goes far beyond the narrow focus of diplomatic ties and foreign policy. Indeed, it concerns the question of the fundamental orientation of Russian society itself. Russian social and political thought has always understood the concept of "Europe" not only in a geographic sense, but also as encompassing a specific culture and civilization. As noted in the first chapter, for the Russian, Europe has often been synonymous with a certain system of political and economic principles, a certain set of moral values, and a certain cultural space. Arguments about our relationship to European civilization always reflect the ongoing debates involving European interdependence, Russia's distinct national character, and Russia's historical path of development.

For most of their history, Russians have continually pondered the question "Are we are part of Europe?" Regardless of the answer, it is undeniable that the European vector has played the lead role in determining Russia's foreign policy for the past several centuries. In fact,

Russia did not just meet Europe halfway, but has consistently acted as an integral part of Europe's system of foreign relations. At every major turning point in the continent's history—be it the defeat of Napoleon's empire or the formation of the Entente alliance—Russia has played an active and indispensable part in the European concert, and has been an integral part of the overall European balance.

In the twentieth century Russia's role in European affairs increased even more, despite the ideological, military, and political backlash throughout much of Europe in response to the tremors of revolution in Russia. Our country's victory over fascism in World War II allowed us to participate in building the postwar European security architecture. And despite the Iron Curtain, the USSR and the countries of Europe developed a wide array of political, economic, cultural, and other kinds of contacts during the cold war. The Soviet Union's initiative and participation in European affairs gave rise to the trend toward détente, and subsequently toward pan-European security and cooperation, culminating in the signing of the Helsinki Final Act in 1975. Finally, the fundamental changes in our country have placed Europe at the epicenter of a radical shift in world affairs, symbolized by the fall of the Berlin Wall and the reunification of Germany.

Of course, the stormy events of the second half of the twentieth century have resulted in significant alterations to Europe's international role. Having to a large degree forfeited its ability to effect change in the world, Europe nevertheless continues to maintain its place as the world's leading intellectual and cultural center. No less important, Europe continues to develop its political and economic potential. For many regions around the globe, the Old World of Europe is a model of development and integration that demonstrates a remarkable capacity for self-renewal, relying upon the firm bases of partnership and mediation to resolve international issues.

As the grandfather of modern international law, Europe received, after the end of the cold war, a unique opportunity to use its own positive example to reaffirm the primacy of law and world culture in interstate dealings. The prerequisites for this were established in November 1990, with the adoption of the Charter of Paris for a New Europe. The participating states undertook "to build, consolidate, and strengthen democracy as the only system of government of [their] nations." They expressed their resolve to observe human rights, including the right to participate in free and fair elections and the right to fair and public trial if charged with an offense. Among their overall goals, the participants of this pan-European process identified the development of market economies, adherence to the rule of law, and respect for the rights of the individual.

The Charter of Paris provided, for the first time in European history, the opportunity to realize the goal of building a unified, democratic Europe. In reality, however, this goal has turned out to be much more difficult to attain. Certainly, in the past decade Europe has made substantial progress toward the creation of a unified environment of stability and security, of economic prosperity and lasting democracy. Europe had gained more than any other region of the world from the end of cold war–era confrontation. The destruction of the Iron Curtain opened up unprecedented opportunities for cooperation and rapprochement between states and peoples with shared democratic values.

Nevertheless, the final goal of a unified "Super Europe" remains as remote as ever. The main reason for this is that the processes of security and economic integration developed during this time were based on structures shared by only a few European states. The push to expand NATO, and the alliance's military action against Yugoslavia in the spring of 1999, demonstrated the very real danger that new lines of division would be drawn across Europe. It also jeopardized the existing international legal basis for European cooperation.

It is clear that such a trend could only serve to weaken the European continent's role in international affairs. In many instances, other regions—Southeast Asia and Latin America, for example—have shown a much higher level of political unity and harmony in key areas of international interaction than has been demonstrated by Europe. The potential contained in the pan-European structure, especially in the Organization for Security and Cooperation in Europe, has scarcely been tapped and is sometimes, apparently, consciously ignored.

Russia formulates its policy toward Europe based on the conviction that Europe can and should become the starting point for universal strategic stability across the globe. First and foremost, this requires substantial progress in disarmament, coupled with the preservation and consolidation of current treaties and agreements in this area. Moscow values highly the fact that many leading European countries joined with an overwhelming majority of the world community to call for protection of the system of international and bilateral disarmament treaties developed over the past thirty years. There is reason to hope that this view will be reflected not simply in rhetoric, but in actual European interaction.

Europe's potential for resolving other critical issues of the modern world goes underused, in particular, in regulating regional conflict. As a cosponsor of the Middle East peace process, Russia feels it is essential to actively engage the international mediation efforts of the European Union. Indeed, Moscow's approach to peace in the Middle East is so similar to that of Brussels, that Russia and the EU could work toward this end in greater concert or even, if need be, jointly. Undoubtedly, there are also real opportunities for closer cooperation between European states and other regions of the world, including the Mediterranean, the Far East, and Asia as a whole.

One of the fundamental tenets of Russia's European policy is the expansion of bilateral relations with individual countries. Here, the main point is that for all the twists and turns of Europe's stormy history, bilateral cooperation has always been a positive stabilizing factor in international relations in Europe.

Russia will continue to increase interaction with Western Europe. Over the past decade, Russia's relations with virtually all of these countries have been taken to a qualitatively new level. We have become privileged partners in our cooperative efforts with such countries as Germany, Italy, Great Britain, France, Spain, and others. We feel this is exceptionally valuable.

Regarding relations with Central and Eastern Europe, the updated Foreign Policy Concept of Russia states: "It is vital to maintain traditional economic ties and expand humanitarian and cultural cooperation, to resolve the present crisis situations, and to put more effort into cooperation in response to new conditions and in keeping with Russia's national interests." The Concept also points out the possibilities for rewarding cooperation between Russia and Lithuania, Latvia, and Estonia: "Russia favors a good-neighborly approach and mutually beneficial cooperation in relations with these countries. An indispensable condition here is respect by those states of the Russian interests, including in the key question of respect for the rights of the Russian-speaking population."

On the whole, there is no European country with which Russia has insurmountable differences or quarrels that would preclude open relations and mutual cooperation. There are no obstacles to create truly pan-European interaction on key issues of peace and international stability. For Europe to play an active role in forming a new system of international relations based on equal rights and democracy, it must first become an influential pole. Speaking in the German Bundestag in September 2001, President Putin emphasized that Europe would be able to strengthen its reputation as a powerful and truly independent center for world politics only by joining with Russia to combine fully the resources at Europe's disposal—human, territorial, natural, economic, and cultural—as well as its defense capabilities, with those of Russia. This is what it will take to build a "Greater Europe" with a unified area of stability and security, economic prosperity, and permanent democracy, as a precursor of a unified and secure world.

The main goal of Russia's European policy is to work toward a stable, nondiscriminatory, and universal system for European security. The basis for such a system was established a quarter of a century ago by the historic Helsinki Final Act. The underlying principles put forth in the act and agreed on by all signatory parties correspond fully to the UN Charter and to universally held principles of international law.

If creating a pan-European system of security is Europe's primary developmental goal, then the personification of this goal is the Organization for Security and Cooperation in Europe. As the only body to unite all European states, it has the capability to put into practice the principle of equal and guaranteed security for all states, regardless of their membership in a military or political union or in any other exclusive group. From the moment the Conference on Security and Cooperation in Europe was transformed into its analogous institution (the OSCE) in 1994, Russia has continuously called for the organization's support and transformation into a full-scale regional body. The OSCE must become the forum in which the European states can hammer out a joint approach to today's main problems and which will be the common voice in dialogues with other regional organizations. This is the OSCE's primary political function, and it must be supported and developed. Moreover, this would represent a substantial step toward a new structure for international relations as outlined in the previous chapter, one based on the interaction of the leading regional organizations, on leadership by the UN, and on absolute adherence to international law.

During the period of its existence, the OSCE has undergone enormous organizational development and has accumulated a wealth of experience in negotiating consensus positions among all its member-states. At its Budapest summit in December 1994, the OSCE created new components: the Secretariat; the Council, made up of foreign ministers; the Parliamentary Assembly; the Center for Conflict Resolution; and the Bureau for Free Elections (which later became the Bureau on Democratic Institutions and Human Rights).[9] The Budapest summit approved a new edition of the Vienna Document on Confidence and Security Building Measures, which stipulates that signatories provide a wider range of information on their military forces, on defense planning, and on defense spending. In the Lisbon Declaration on a Common and Comprehensive Security Model for Europe for the Twenty-First Century (December 1996), the heads of state and representatives of OSCE member-states affirmed the universal and indivisible nature of security on the European continent.

In preparing for the OSCE summit in Istanbul (held in mid-November 1999), Russia faced a complex diplomatic challenge. As always, we sought to advocate our wide-ranging foreign policy interests and to adopt documents that were acceptable to us and that, in this case, could lay a solid foundation for European security in the twenty-first century. However, we could not allow the summit to turn into an ad hoc court, putting Russia on trial for its involvement in Chechnya. This required efforts to keep the meeting on a constructive course and avoid any conflict with the West. On the whole, we were able to accomplish this. In the end, the Istanbul summit represented a landmark in the OSCE's history. Although the meeting received one-sided attention from the international media, it produced some serious and far-reaching decisions that every citizen of Europe should be aware of.

The main political outcome of the summit was a promise by all OSCE members to adhere to the principles contained in the UN Charter and in the Helsinki Accord. This meant that interstate relations in Europe would continue to be based on the principles of equal sovereignty, inviolability of borders, territorial integrity of states, peaceful settlement of disputes, noninterference in internal affairs, and respect for human rights. These principles are the building blocks for Europe's future security and stability.

Russia conducts ongoing diplomatic efforts to support the OSCE's efforts to achieve progress in security policy, an area in which we feel that the organization has scarcely begun to exploit its potential. The OSCE has the capability to take on in the future the role of coordinating a European security system and incorporating input from other bodies with relevant experience and abilities. It is also necessary to further develop the OSCE's mechanisms for evaluating security in various ways and to more fully use the OSCE Forum on Cooperation in this area. The Istanbul resolutions—the Platform for Cooperative Security as outlined in the Charter for European Security, in particular—lay out a clear road map for the OSCE to develop along this path.[10]

Still, we cannot close our eyes to the substantial obstacles that block further strengthening of the OSCE. Recently, the West has tried to restrict the OSCE's functions and turn the organization into a kind of provincial forum, with its scope limited primarily to humanitarian responsibilities. This tack was obvious during the November 2000 session of the OSCE Council of Foreign Ministers (CFM) in Vienna.

There is a danger that the OSCE will be transformed from a pan-European institution for formulating and expressing the collective will of all its member-states into an instrument for exerting influence on specific states, a kind of tool for "forced democratization." Attempts to limit the OSCE's sphere of work to humanitarian and human rights issues clearly result from a drive to build European security around exclusive organizations and unions, chiefly NATO. Russia believes this approach is misguided. It is directly at odds with the fundamental responsibilities of the OSCE's role and runs counter to the basic direction in which European security is headed, as outlined by the Istanbul charter. The dynamic of European and global interaction is such that creating a new architecture for security and stability on the continent cannot be the privilege of a "chosen" group of states. History has shown repeatedly that outside attempts to force any state to accept arrangements made without its input are doomed to fail.

This organizational crisis began to be evident at the OSCE-CFM session held in Bucharest on December 3–4, 2001, causing growing concern among the member-states. As a result, several important documents were approved, including one on fighting international terrorism, which clearly indicates the great untapped potential of this unique body.[11]

The Council of Europe is called on to make an important contribution toward the creation of a Greater Europe, united by common democratic values. Founded on May 5, 1949, the Council of Europe's self-described primary goal is to achieve unity among Europeans for advancing the ideals and principles of pluralistic democracy, human rights, and the rule of law, and to foster economic and social progress in Europe.[12] But with the cold war and effective rift in the continent, the council was unable to complete its mission for all of Europe.

In the second half of the 1980s, the political landscape of Europe began to undergo some fundamental changes, which, in turn, gave the Council of Europe a new dynamic. By opening its doors to young new democracies, the council had the opportunity to really assist Europeans to "join together to build Greater Europe without dividing lines."

The Russian Federation's entry into the Council of Europe on February 28, 1996, helped turn the council into a truly pan-European institution.[13] This move was a conscious strategic decision made by Russia's leadership, by the Federal Assembly, and by politically active citizens' groups. At its core is the conviction that membership in the council helps establish and strengthen the institutions of democracy and law in Russia and supports basic human rights and freedoms. These are some of the things that have been achieved in hard-won reforms and are most important to Russians.

There were those who doubted the wisdom of Russia's entry into the council, fearing that in its present condition Russia would be unable to fulfill the responsibilities that come with membership. They did not want

Russia to come under criticism or be sanctioned. These fears have generally not been realized, even in spite of the "Chechnya cult" of the council's Parliamentary Assembly.

The fact that Russia has adopted recognized European legal standards and is a member of twenty-eight European conventions had enormous significance in the formation of a government based on law and on the development of civil society in Russia.[14] Specifically, this has been important in government and society for the defense of human rights and the rights of ethnic minorities, in education, in culture, and in sports. These are all areas in which Russia intends to sign nearly a dozen European legal and diplomatic acts. Some of these stipulate that member-states will accept international monitoring mechanisms, such as the European Court on Human Rights. Monitoring of this nature provides an added guarantee for democracy and the rule of law. Although the formation of a stable socioeconomic base for personal freedoms has turned out to be more difficult than it seemed in the early 1990s, on the whole, Russian society has firmly accepted the primacy of human rights and the need to defend them, even by international means, if necessary. The dramatic events of the past decade have shown that even in the most difficult moments, Russians have never doubted the need for free elections, separation of powers, or freedom of speech. More and more, we see ourselves as part of the democratic civilized community of European states.

Russia values highly the ability to access the rich experience and intellectual legacy of the Council of Europe. Much of this can be utilized as we continue the process of democratization in our country. At the same time, thanks in large part to the council, other Europeans are gaining more access to and a better understanding of Russian ideas and initiatives.

By fulfilling its responsibilities as a new member of the Council of Europe, Russia makes valuable contributions to the organization's efforts and plays an important initiatory role in the organization's further development. A priority for Russia is supporting the "spirit of Strasbourg," expressed at the Council's second summit. Strasbourg stands for the unification of Europe, not the erection of new barriers. It stands for the rule of law expanding to cover the continent, and not the rule of force and its attendant military institutions. In this connection we welcome the political declaration adopted by the Council's Ministerial Committee at the

104th session in Budapest—"Greater Europe without Dividing Lines"—which takes Europe closer to unification.[15]

At the same time, Russia does not hide its disapproval of various prejudices and double standards that exist in the council. In particular, the organization's position regarding the NATO bombing of Yugoslavia in effect justified this illegal action. By contrast, the Parliamentary Assembly made an entirely subjective evaluation of Russia's actions in Chechnya and continues to stand idly by as human rights and the rights of ethnic minorities are violated in Latvia and Estonia. Russian diplomacy constantly emphasizes that the Council of Europe can remain true to the traditions of European humanism, in which the individual is the measure of all things, only by conducting more effective human rights monitoring that includes the rights of thousands of individuals without citizenship in the Baltic states. In particular, the council could make more use of its relevant bodies, especially the European Commission against Racism and Intolerance and the Commissariat for Human Rights. These bodies should take action to ensure that the human rights situation of Russian-speaking populations in Latvia and Estonia fully conforms to accepted European standards. This is a matter of active diplomacy for Russia.

One of the council's more serious responsibilities, directly related to the organization's mission, is to assist new member-states in their internal reforms and, by doing so, to equalize levels of democratization across all parts of Europe. This is an important component of stability on the continent and an effective antidote for conflict situations of various kinds. However, the council could also become more active in the social and economic arena. It is no secret that in Europe today ideological barriers have been replaced by the new dividing lines of economics—especially the distinction between members of the European Union (EU), countries invited to join, and those left on the sidelines—as well as the gap between haves and have-nots within European countries. This is why the slogan voiced from the podium at the council's second summit about social unity across the continent—both between and within the countries of Europe—must not be left on paper. The council should take specific action to bring this slogan to life and put it into practice. Any such actions would be fully supported by the council's own Social Charter and by other international instruments.[16]

Finally, the ideas of Jean Monnet, one of the Council of Europe's founding ideologists, bear repeating. Monnet said that a unified Europe should not be simply a "Europe of coal and steel," meaning that the loss of culture was unforgivable. Russia continues to work to increase the council's role in developing cultural cooperation across Europe.

Thus, the Council of Europe has every opportunity to become—together with the OSCE—one of the pillars of the new European architecture and to play a key role in ensuring the democratic, social, and economic components of European security. In shaping Europe's legal, social, and cultural space today, the Council of Europe paves the way for full political interaction between all nationals, from one end of Europe to the other.

The European Union has an important role to play in strengthening security and developing cooperation in Europe. Logically, this is so because as integration across Europe deepens, the EU will be an increasingly important factor in European and world politics.

Many vigorous processes are at work within the EU today. The EU continues to expand its borders, the euro has been adopted as a common currency, and finally, many new integrated structures are being established in politics, the military, health care, and other areas. It is obvious that these processes are already having effects across the continent and will in many ways change the shape of Europe in the twenty-first century.

Russia sees multilateral cooperation with the EU as a priority and seeks to raise such cooperation to the level of a strategic partnership. Moreover, the EU is today one of Russia's most important partners in political dialogue, as well as in trade and economics, finance, and investment. In his message to the Russian Federation's Federal Meeting in 2001, President Putin noted the growing significance of our efforts to effectively partner with the EU and emphasized that "Russia's course toward integration with Europe will become one of the key areas of Russian foreign policy."

The Agreement on Partnership and Cooperation between Russia and the European Union, which went into effect in December 1997, has had a positive effect on Russia's ties to EU member-states.[17] As yet, only the first steps have been taken in exploiting the rich potential of this agreement. The opposing strategies each of us have for development ensure that our relations will continue to be quite dynamic in nature.

President Putin approved the Russian Federation's strategy for relations with the EU for the midrange future in June 2000. The strategy addresses many interconnected issues related to Russia's status as an independent pole in a multipolar world and to bilateral cooperation and partnership between Russia and the EU.

Russia's strategy calls for several things:

—expanding the format of political dialogue between Russia and the EU and increasing the dialogue's effectiveness

—developing mutual trade and joint investment, and cooperation in finance

—protecting Russia's interests as the EU expands

—developing a pan-European structure for cooperation

—increasing Russian-EU cooperation in science and technology

—expanding transnational and inter-regional ties

—bringing economic legislation and technical standards closer together

If programs are carried out in these areas, cooperation between Russia and the EU would be taken to a qualitatively new level.

The development of a unified policy for security and defense is a new direction for the EU. In general, the urge for Europeans to rely on their own forces to ensure their security and deal with crisis situations is completely logical, and Russia is prepared to work constructively with them in this context. Russia and the EU are natural partners in the search for joint responses to the new threats and challenges faced by European and international security. This potential for cooperation must be realized in the interest of strengthening global peace and regional security, and based on strict adherence to the basic principles of international law.

This approach was formulated and adopted at the Russia-EU summit in Paris on October 30, 2000, as the Joint Declaration on Strengthening Dialogue and Cooperation on Political and Security Matters in Europe, which forms the basis for bilateral interaction on security and defense. In accordance with this agreement, a mechanism for special consultation on security and defense matters is being instituted, and the spectrum of consultation and strategic dialogue on disarmament issues is being expanded. It was also resolved to promote cooperation in operational crisis management and to examine mechanisms for Russia to contribute to the European Union's operations. Obviously, all of this requires creating an appropriate legal base and the mechanisms for taking each side's interests into account.[18]

The creation of the post of EU high representative for the Common Foreign and Security Policy and its close connection to the secretary general of the Western European Union also provides new opportunities for international cooperation. Russia is prepared to work together with the EU on a wide range of issues of strategic stability, disarmament, elimination of weapons of mass destruction, and regional security. We are also open to interacting with the EU not only within Europe, but anywhere that our cooperative efforts might yield a positive contribution to the strengthening of international security and stability.

To put it succinctly, Russia is carefully following the development of integration efforts within the European Union, especially in areas where common approaches for member-states to address the most urgent European and international issues are being formulated. Russia is not disinterested, since these processes are creating a fundamentally new structure for international relations in Europe.

Speaking at the EU summit in Stockholm on March 23, 2001, President Putin explained that joining the EU is not a goal for Russia, either now or in the foreseeable future. However, we cannot stand on the sidelines and simply watch the wide-scale integration of our continent. It is interesting to note that as the eighteenth century was ending and the nineteenth century began, European political thought produced various plans for building a unified Europe and transforming European society.[19] As long ago as that, and despite the wide variety of ways in which European intellectuals perceived Russia during the Enlightenment, every one of these unification schemes described some kind of specific role and place for Russia. In today's globalized environment, close interaction between Russia and the EU can be a powerful stabilizing factor that would not only greatly expand the horizons of security and cooperation on the continent, but would also guarantee unified Europe an influential place in world politics. Russia is prepared to proceed in this direction, in the context of a strategic partnership.

NATO continues to have a noticeable influence both inside Europe and beyond its borders. Despite all the rhetoric about its "transformation," the organization remains primarily a military bloc. This is one of the realities in Europe today.

During the past ten years, the Russian leadership has invested considerable effort in improving the Russian public's perception of NATO, a perception that was heavily clouded by the cold war. Russia has taken major steps toward rapprochement with NATO, through bilateral relations and as part of the Partnership for Peace program. In May 1997, Russia and the alliance signed the Founding Act on Mutual Relations, Cooperation, and Security.[20] On the basis of this document, Russia and NATO formed the Permanent Joint Council (PJC) to examine security-related issues of mutual concern. The PJC has provided a context for useful discussions on such issues as security in Europe, nonproliferation of weapons of mass destruction, regulation of regional conflict, and peace making. NATO and Russia have also cooperated militarily, both in Bosnia and in emergency planning and disaster relief.

Unfortunately, these efforts were seriously undermined by NATO's expansion to the East and, especially, by the alliance's aggression against the sovereign nation of Yugoslavia. And NATO's new strategic concept demonstrates how the alliance continues to be wedded to Europe's past rather than to its future. Nevertheless, Russia has once again taken a pragmatic approach to its relationship with NATO and is focused on fostering dialogue and cooperation in areas of mutual interest.

The meeting of the Permanent Joint Council at the Level of Foreign Ministers in Brussels on December 7, 2001, can be considered a major turning point in relations between NATO and Russia. The council decided to "give new impetus and substance to the partnership, with the goal of creating a new council bringing together the 19 NATO member-states and Russia to identify and pursue opportunities for joint action 'at 20.'" It was also resolved to intensify cooperation in the struggle against terrorism and in other areas, including crisis management, nonproliferation, arms control and confidence building measures, theatre missile defense, search and rescue at sea, and civil emergencies and disaster relief. This represents a major step toward a qualitatively new relationship between Russia and NATO, a relationship that will help ensure stability and security in the Euro-Atlantic area.

Obviously, no system of European security can be stable unless we find effective means to deal with localized tension and conflict on the continent, especially in the Balkans. Today we have the unique opportunity to show solidarity with the new leadership of Yugoslavia, to help to strengthen democracy in this country through our joint efforts. This can only help the cause of security and stability throughout the entire Balkan region. It is urgent that we work to restore the ruined economy of the Federal Republic of Yugoslavia. Despite its own economic difficulties, Russia is attempting to provide assistance to the people of Serbia.

It is also obvious that the future of democracy in Yugoslavia will in large part depend on the situation in Kosovo. Unfortunately, much of what has been done up to now under the cover of international structures deployed in the area has actually strengthened the position of the separatists. Events in southern Serbia and in Macedonia during 2001 are an example of this. Kosovo has become the primary threat to regional security and the main source of instability, crime, and terrorism in the south of Europe.

Today, it is difficult to predict the final outcome of the drama unfolding in Kosovo. One thing is clear: a precedent is being created in this area that is being carefully watched from other corners of the planet. If the Kosovo separatists are successful in breaking away from Yugoslavia, then militant separatism and extremism—in the Balkans or anywhere else— will have been given a powerful shot in the arm. I am convinced that this potential outcome is directly at odds with the interests of the entire international community.

We have reached a moment of truth in the Balkans. The states in this region, with the assistance of the international community, may once and for all acknowledge each other's sovereignty and territorial integrity and may cooperate with each other against separatism and terrorism. If this does not come to pass, a new explosion in the Balkans is inevitable. There are no other alternatives. Recent dramatic events in Macedonia are convincing proof of this.

Developments affecting the stability of the Balkans also have an effect on the Mediterranean region, which is sensitive to crisis in both Southern Europe and in the Middle East. The historic fragility and vulnerability of security in the Mediterranean region demands delicate and complex attention. Any effective strategy for strengthening regional security in the area must be based on the concept of an open "Greater Mediterranean," a concept that asserts the principle of multilateral partnership and cooperation between the states of the Mediterranean and Black Sea basins, Southern Europe, and the Middle East.

The various regional and subregional initiatives developed in the Mediterranean must keep this principle in view, and this is especially true for the Euro-Mediterranean Partnership (also known as the Barcelona Process). Despite its difficulty in achieving tangible results so far, this initiative is gaining momentum and will directly improve the situation in the region. Currently, the partnership is preparing its Euro-Mediterranean Charter for Peace and Stability. Participation in this process by any interested country would only be for the better. Russia could make an important contribution to this document, which will stand as the code of conduct for Mediterranean states into the twenty-first century. Its contents, of course, should be in line with the OSCE's Charter for European Security.

No less urgent is the task of building confidence and security in the Mediterranean with regard to naval activity. In particular, at issue here are prior announcement of certain kinds of naval activity, annual exchanges of plans for maneuvers, observation, and increasing cooperation between navies. Vigorous international and cooperative efforts are needed to avoid the proliferation in the Mediterranean of the deadliest kinds of weapons. The idea of a zone free of weapons of mass destruction and the means of their delivery in the Middle East deserves the utmost support.

In contrast to the often complex and contradictory processes at work in Southern Europe, Northern Europe is a model of effective and mutually beneficial regional cooperation. Even during the cold war, Northern Europe enjoyed a higher degree of stability and cooperation than other parts of the Old World. New conditions in Europe have opened up the broadest range of possibilities for international cooperation. After all, this region is full of large and small states with intertwined interests, even if they differ widely in both their political and economic orientations, and also in their conceptions of national security. Because of this, it is precisely in Northern Europe that an effective part of the pan-European system of security and cooperation may be worked out. The prerequisites for this model are already at hand: a history of stability and absence of conflict, and advanced international cooperation between regional organizations—the Council of the Baltic Sea States (CBSS) and the Barents Euro-Arctic Council (BEAC).

Moreover, Northern Europe has a long and unique history of broad cooperation among states as equals, united by a common geography and history, a mutual tendency to form strong relations, and an inclination to seek joint responses to modern challenges. The example of this region should convince all Europeans that security, stability, and prosperity can be achieved through broad international cooperation based on equality. Russia sees this as the primary political goal of the "Northern Dimension," which was initiated at the Feira European Council in June 2000.

History has provided an opportunity to bring together unique economic, scientific, intellectual, and natural resources for the purpose of harmonious and cooperative development in Europe, to raise the standard of living for those who live here, and to solve some of our most serious socioeconomic and environmental problems. We must not let this opportunity pass. The Northern Dimension offers the possibility to make substantial progress in pushing forward cooperation in trade, finance, industrial, and interregional mutual assistance. Even if the immediate beneficiaries of these results are found only in northern Europe, the scale of the projects now under way is so vast that all Europeans will benefit from them in some manner. For instance, the transportation and energy arteries being developed will serve the entire continent.

Russia's contribution to the Northern Dimension could potentially be substantial. Russia has something of value to offer, and not just enormous natural reserves of ore, lumber, oil, and gas. We also possess an extensive scientific and industrial complex, a highly skilled work force, and modern technology. Russia would like to throw itself wholeheartedly into the modernization of its industrial, agricultural, social, and cultural spheres and into the conversion of defense industries and military installations. We have many problems that need immediate attention; in particular, we face ecological issues and dangers from nuclear industry and radiation. So, for Russia, the Northern Dimension is seen as a long-range complex partnership where all these factors come into play. In other words, the more the Northern Dimension concept reflects Russia's needs, the fuller and more extensive will be our participation in it.[21]

The degree to which the integration of Northern Europe and the Baltic meshes with Russia's priorities will depend significantly on how further expansion of the European Union is carried out. It is expected that Poland and the Baltic nations will join the EU soon. This raises two important points that demand attention. First, the Kaliningrad *oblast* will become a Russian enclave within the European Union. This new context will require a model for the socioeconomic development and support of Kaliningrad as a subject of the Russian Federation, that also incorporates beneficial cooperation with the EU and fully respects Russia's interests. Kaliningrad could potentially become an outpost for economic cooperation between Russia and European nations. These issues are already under active discussion between Russia and the EU.

With the proposed entry of Poland and the Baltic states into the EU, the future of a multilateral association like the Council of Baltic Sea States takes on a new light. It will become even more important for the council to clearly define its mission after EU expansion, so that the CBSS can retain its independence and its identity as cooperation expands in the region. Today, Northern Europe has the unique opportunity to develop a stable framework for long-range, mutually beneficial cooperation—the chance must be used wisely.

In the final analysis, Europe will certainly continue to be a priority in Russian foreign policy for a long time to come. Europe enters the new century having eliminated the threat of wide-scale military conflict, and for the first time in its history, all its constituent nations are now moving forward on the basis of shared democratic values. Ahead lies no less complicated a challenge: to become the driving force for the creation of a fair and democratic world order, a force that is able to bring prosperity and stability to the world. This noble goal is only achievable through the combined efforts of all Europeans and through the formation on the European continent of a modern, firm, and stable architecture for security—and on its base, an atmosphere of trust and cooperation. Anything less will not allow us to build a Greater Europe.

The United States

Fundamental changes in the international arena during the 1990s put the United States in the position of a power that had pulled far ahead of its peers in many basic ways: militarily, financially, and economically, and in science and technology. French foreign minister Hubert Védrine coined the term "hyperpower" to describe the contemporary United States.

However, as world events show, even this seemingly enormous advantage does not equate to unconditional leadership in the world. The fabric of modern international relations is too complex and finely woven to be controlled by a single tailor. Today, no one country has the ability to single-handedly contain a regional conflict. This is clear from events in the Middle East over the past few years.

It is also a generally accepted fact that Russian-American relations continue to have a substantial influence on the world's political climate. Russia and the United States, as permanent members of the UN Security Council and the two largest nuclear powers, bear particular responsibility for upholding international peace and security. Both states have global interests, conduct foreign policy along multiple alignments, work to limit and reduce weapons of mass destruction, and actively strive to bring conflict situations under control all over the world. Today, there is scarcely a single important global problem that can be solved without involving both Moscow and Washington.

Nevertheless, the character and content of Russian-American relations have changed radically. Relations between Russia and the United States no longer follow the logic of confrontation leading to hard-line military and political clashes. Our nations no longer see each other as adversaries, and the combined potential of Russia and the United States is great enough to be the deciding factor in the quest for global security and strategic stability.

Of course, this potential can only be realized through equal partnership and by taking each other's interests into account, and only within the context of broad international cooperation. It is fundamentally important that this approach was reflected in the Joint Statement on Common Security Challenges at the Threshold of the Twenty-First Century signed by Presidents Boris Yeltsin and Bill Clinton on September 2, 1998, in Moscow. The statement clearly states that "the common security challenges on the threshold of the twenty-first century can be met only by consistently mobilizing the efforts of the entire international community." This joint communiqué also emphasizes that "the United States of America and the Russian Federation are natural partners in advancing international peace and stability." It stresses that Russia and the United States will continue to play leadership roles "in both bilateral and multilateral settings" to reach our common security goals.

World events over the past decade have created a situation in which the global interests of Russia and the United States have not always coincided, and in fact, sometimes have been in opposition. This has generally been the case in instances when Washington was inclined to act unilaterally, not only by dictating its will to sovereign states, but by sidestepping international standards in order to use force against them.

Moscow's and Washington's divergent understandings of the world following the cold war have, to a certain extent, affected the quality of bilateral relations between them. Russia, having undergone a deep internal political and social transformation, has made a decisive break from the stereotypes of confrontation. We have begun to chart our course in international affairs with a steady eye on the creation of a new democratic world order. Moscow has sincerely sought an equal partnership with the United States; this is in our national interest. After all, it is obvious that long-term confrontation with the United States, especially a military or technical confrontation, would seriously complicate Russia's development. Moreover it would hinder our progress toward achieving a stable economy. The development of U.S. policy, however, has largely been influenced by the mentality of a "victor" in the cold war. This view clearly denigrates the role of the UN and is reflected by a strong urge to act outside the bounds of commonly recognized international law. It belies a tendency toward coercion, up to and including the use of force, particularly in the Persian Gulf and in the Balkans. A new irritant in Russian-U.S. relations has been the U.S. attempt to force Russia out of territories that formed part of the Soviet Union (such as the Caspian Sea basin), claiming that such areas now form zones of "vital American interest," even to the point of bringing in military infrastructure. This is a clear case of Washington's overestimation of its own abilities and its disinclination to take into account the new, objective imperative that is taking shape in contemporary international affairs.

All of this engendered the familiar zigzags in Russian-American relations during the 1990s. However, in moments of truth, realism took the upper hand. When something vital was at stake, both sides understood that the sphere of their mutual interests in today's world was greater than that of their differences, and that in the larger strategic issues of peace and stability, they were partners rather than adversaries. Moscow and Washington gradually developed a new style of interaction that acknowledged each other's interests and mutual desire to overcome these hurdles, and so preserve a positive outlook in Russian-American relations. This understanding allowed Moscow and Washington to begin an intense, summit-level dialogue during the 1990s. In 2000 alone, President Putin met President Bill Clinton four times. And President Putin has met with President George W. Bush four times during the new administration's first year.

The central theme for U.S.-Russian relations remains the reduction of nuclear weapons. After all, our two countries entered the 1990s each with arsenals of between 11,000 and 12,000 strategic nuclear warheads. After the cold war had lost its logic and the nature of the relationship between Russia and the United States began to change fundamentally, such large arsenals were an anachronism. Therefore, the Strategic Arms Reduction Treaty (START I) was a product of its time. This treaty was signed in Moscow on July 31, 1991, went into effect December 5, 1994, and stipulated that over the following seven years, each side would reduce the number of its strategic launch vehicles to 1,600 and the number of its nuclear warheads to 6,000. Overall, START I reduced the combined nuclear capability of Russia and the United States by 40 percent. Moscow has fully complied with the reductions stipulated in the treaty and expects that Washington will do the same.

The next significant step for Moscow and Washington in nuclear disarmament was START II, signed on January 3, 1993, which stipulated further reductions in strategic arms to a total of between 3,000 and 3,500 warheads for each side. In addition, because of delays in ratification, the two parties decided in 1997 to extend the period for achieving the reductions to December 31, 2007. Unfortunately, because of Washington's current position, START II and the 1997 protocol have not gone into effect. Russia, on the other hand, ratified these documents in April 2000.

In accordance with agreements between the Russian and U.S. presidents made in August 1999, reviews have been conducted on implementation details for START III, which should lead to further strategic offensive weapons reductions on both sides. At first, in accordance with the March 1997 joint declaration by Presidents Yeltsin and Clinton, the target for each party was to achieve a ceiling of 2,000–2,500 strategic nuclear weapons by December 31, 2007. Subsequently, as described above, President Putin proposed in November 2000 that this number be lowered even further: to 1,500 or less on each side. The U.S. administration countered the proposal with its own numbers. A bit earlier, we had given to the Americans—at the Okinawa G-8 summit—our proposals for START III implementation, which included measures to ensure transparency and adherence, encompass the full range of types of strategic nuclear arms, promote the irreversibility of deep reductions, and eliminate an entire class of sea-based ballistic missiles, among others.[22] However, a disturbing trend in arms control is the tendency of some in Washington to abandon the process of negotiation in favor of unilateral steps, which are not subject to any of the types of mutually binding legal constraints, like on-site monitoring, that treaties would provide for.

In dragging out efforts to produce new START agreements, the United States will sometimes point to Russia's supposed superiority in the area of nonstrategic nuclear weapons. Here, too, not only is our country open to dialogue, but we have also taken concrete action. Russia has completely removed all tactical nuclear weapons from our surface ships and multipurpose submarines, as well as from our land-based navy aircraft.

One-third of our naval tactical nuclear weapons have been eliminated. We are completing the destruction of all nuclear artillery munitions, nuclear warheads for tactical missiles, and nuclear mines. Half of our Zenith missile nuclear warheads and half of our nuclear bombs have been destroyed.

Another important topic for Russian-American dialogue is cooperation in efforts toward nonproliferation of weapons of mass destruction and the means for their delivery. Cooperation in this area is ongoing and takes the form of a wide range of public and private contacts. The seven joint expert groups on specific export control have done beneficial work in recent years on these issues. Export control is becoming an increasingly important tool in national security and strategic stability efforts.

At the June 2000 Moscow talks, the Russian and U.S. presidents agreed to continue cooperating on nonproliferation issues, which is in the interest of both countries.[23] Simultaneously, the Russian side again clearly stated that this cooperation should not limit the legal rights of our two states to develop multilateral ties with third parties, including military and technology cooperation for peaceful uses of nuclear energy that do not violate present nonproliferation guidelines. Attempts to use sanctions to exert pressure on Russia in any way are deliberately counterproductive and do nothing to strengthen cooperation between our two countries on nonproliferation issues.

Russian-U.S. cooperation plays an enormous role in removing other relics of the cold war era that complicate our relationship. The West's organization for export control of so-called dual-use technologies— COCOM (Coordinating Committee on Multilateral Export Controls)— was superseded by the universal Wassenaar Arrangement,[24] under which, with our participation, all decisions are based on consensus. Russia has joined the Group of 7 and is a member of APEC. The final step of the G-7's expansion into the G-8 took place in Denver in 1997, during the period when the United States served as chair of the group. Russia and the United States have also joined forces to try and coordinate their efforts to achieve reform at the United Nations.

It is no secret that Russia and the United States will, in large part, determine the outcome of the European unification process, especially on the question of whether the Old World's dividing lines between "East" and "West" will be preserved or erased. Russia realizes that the transatlantic relationship is a given, and even has a stabilizing influence. In no way do we advocate that the United States be excluded from Europe, but neither do we want Russia to be relegated to Europe's backyard. The goal of Russian diplomacy is to reliably anchor the transatlantic relationship by providing a balance via the Pacific—ensuring close U.S.-Russian ties by linking California and the West Coast to the Russian Far East.

With goodwill on both sides, much has been accomplished together in the OSCE. It is difficult to imagine how, without coordinated efforts from Moscow and Washington, a detailed, forward-looking document— the Charter for European Security, adopted at the OSCE's Istanbul summit—could have been realized.[25] However, it is also a sad reality that when modern international relations took off their cold war corset, conflict at the regional level began to rise. Without coordinated action from Russia and the United States, these problems cannot be resolved. Moscow and Washington have prior experience in joint efforts to end conflict and promote peace; both sides worked together in the Namibia accords and both served as cosponsors in the Middle East peace process. Today, there are enormous challenges in fulfilling the UN Security Council's Kosovo resolutions, especially now that a democratic leadership has come to power in Belgrade. However, Russian-U.S. cooperative efforts on the issue of Afghanistan have yielded some success, and also are a sign that times are changing. Much remains to be done in countering the new challenges posed by the spread of weapons of mass destruction, transnational crime, and the threat of global financial and economic crisis. Russian-U.S. cooperation in the fight against international terrorism has become a reality, unthinkable during our years of mutual confrontation.

Russian-U.S. economic relations have taken off vigorously. Trade volume has increased, business cooperation has spread and become more diverse, consolidation of the treaty and legal bases for bilateral economic ties continues, and regional contact has intensified. Much of this increase is due to the successful creation of an effective institutional infrastructure that supports the needs of those who engage in cooperative business endeavors between our two countries today. Important steps have been taken toward easing several cold war–era restrictions on economic cooperation. The 1993 U.S. Friendship Act (Public Law 103-199) stipulated the reexamination of over seventy pieces of legislation that discriminated against Russia or former Soviet republics in one way or another. Russia received most-favored-nation status from the United States, which made a significant portion of our trade duty free. With the arrival of the Bush administration, we need to create effective bilateral mechanisms to coordinate efforts for further expanding our trade and economic ties. On the whole, Russian-U.S. economic ties have proved to be "frost-resistant," both during periods of political tension and after the near global financial collapse of 1998. In 2000, the bilateral trade volume stood at approximately $10.2 billion, and Russia's trade surplus reached $5.8 billion.

Cooperation in the area of investment is expanding as well. The United States leads in investment in the Russian economy—more than 35 percent of all foreign direct investment comes from the United States. Most of this goes to the fuel and energy sector, where large-scale joint projects in oil field development are under way, particularly on Sakhalin. Large projects are also being carried out in manufacturing, telecommunications, food processing, tourism and hotels, and financial services. There has been a shift in joint business and economic ventures, whereby the remaining obstacles are now of our own making; that is, political in nature and not related to business. Washington is nearly ready to acknowledge the full market status of our economy. When it does so, this will result in the final elimination of all remaining trade restrictions imposed on Russia.

It is unfortunate but true, however, that some in the United States continue to advocate economic measures as a means of political pressure against Russia. These kinds of connections were widely practiced during the cold war but are inappropriate and doomed to failure today. There are currently very real obstacles to more active business ties, in particular, obstacles standing in the way of large amounts of American investment. We know what these obstacles are and the reforms now under way represent an attempt to address, if not completely eliminate, them.

The main thing is to maintain a positive dynamic and a desire to further Russian-American economic partnership. The main orientation points for continued partnership were outlined in the November 2001 Joint Statement on a New Relationship between the United States and Russia.[26] Of course, each U.S. administration is apt to have a slightly different take on our "new relationship." But when all is said and done, the

United States should be guided by its domestic and foreign economic agendas to help American business seeking to tap into the huge Russian market and gain access to Russia's modern technology and work force.

In the middle of the last century, Chancellor Gorchakov wrote of the United States,

> In our eyes, this Union is more than simply a substantial element in the world's political balance. In addition, it represents a people in whom our sovereign and all of Russia are most cordially interested. Our two countries, situated so distant one from the other in the earlier period of their development, were "chosen" as it were to form a natural solidarity of interests and sympathies that they have already proven to each other.[27]

This thesis holds true today, as well. The philosophy of "pragmatic cooperation" is inexorably—although not always as quickly as one would like—gaining strength in Russian-American relations. This is a completely logical response to the long-range plans of each of our countries. Moreover, the strategic goals of both Russia and the United States in most international issues are close or even coincide. It is another matter that the paths and methods we each propose to reach our goals often differ, which sometimes causes conflict. When this happens, it is essential to approach the situation calmly and to try to maintain a consistent bilateral political dialogue, to seek points in which our positions coincide, to try to resolve our differences with respect for each other's interests and in accordance with international law. There simply is no other way.

It goes without saying that we cannot agree on everything. The fact that Russia and the United States each have their own national interests that are at odds with some of the approaches of the other side is perfectly natural and expected, and should not be harped on. For example, our countries may differ on how best to conduct relations with a particular country in the world. So, we resist when the United States tries to impose its perceptions of "good" or "bad" states. We are against the United States telling us whom we should have relations with and whom we should treat as outcasts, and we are against the most extreme of U.S. actions—the overthrow of a political regime in order to block our relations with a particular state. We conduct our cooperative efforts with third-party countries in strict adherence to existing standards of international law and all recognized international agreements, and we reject any claims by the United States to act as a court of arbitration in this regard. Nor will Russia accept Washington's blatant double standard. This is when a state with whom Moscow one day has been "advised" not to maintain mutually beneficial relations because of supposed "bad behavior," the next day joins the ranks of the United States' partners and its markets are suddenly flooded with American companies.

Some alarming tendencies in bilateral relations were apparent during the second half of the 1990s and at the beginning of the present decade. Certain forces in Washington, having wagered on global hegemony, were prepared to sacrifice the long-term benefits of cooperation with Russia in order to achieve this goal. To further this cause, they unabashedly made use of the U.S. presidential campaign, and the American media unfurled an anti-Russian campaign unprecedented in the post–cold war era for its scale and viciousness. As a result, it must be acknowledged that Russian-U.S. relations had a rocky start when the new Republican administration took power. Washington undertook a series of antagonistic steps toward Russia, including the unwarranted expulsion of a large group of Russian diplomats. The Russian side, following its principled line of protecting its national interests, responded accordingly. However, ongoing contacts between Presidents Vladimir Putin and George W. Bush conveyed Moscow's understanding that only mutually beneficial dialogue, as equals, and realistic interaction between Russia and the United States can effectively counter the new challenges and threats we face today. Over time, Washington displayed signs that it, too, was coming round to this realization. Moreover, the tragic events of September 11, 2001, have underscored the importance and urgency of our cooperation.

I am convinced that today it is in the interest neither of Russia nor of the United States to weaken the other or undermine the other's position or role in the world. President Bush said it quite simply on May 1, 2001: "The cold war is over." It has become a thing of the past, and a new era is upon us. Russia fully understands the changes that have swept over the world and we are strengthening the foundation of our renewed relationship accordingly. Speaking at an October 2001 joint press conference with President Bush in Shanghai, President Putin remarked on the future of Russian-American relations, "in the century to come, our strategic priority is long-term partnership—partnership based on the common values of world civilization, and partnership that works toward the common goals of global development and progress. This is the direction in which we intend to move forward." This basic approach was reflected in the joint statement on the new relationship between the United States and Russia, mentioned above, adopted at a Russian-American summit meeting in Washington. This document states that

> our countries [Russia and the United States] are embarked on a new relationship for the twenty-first century, founded on a commitment to the values of democracy, the free market, and the rule of law. The United States and Russia have overcome the legacy of the cold war. . . . [W]e are determined to work together, and with other nations and international organizations, including the United Nations, to promote security, economic well-being, and a peaceful, prosperous, free world.

We were not surprised by Washington's decision to withdraw from the 1972 ABM Treaty. But we feel that this step is a mistake. In addition, the present high level of relations between our countries must not merely be maintained, but should be used to quickly develop a new framework for strategic interrelations.

On the whole, it is in Russia's interests for the United States to continue to play an active role in the international community's efforts to ensure a stable and orderly global society, and to facilitate development of a progressive world financial and economic system. This would give Russia and the United States expanded opportunities for interaction at the international level. Life itself dictates the need for pragmatic, constructive, and predictable relations between Moscow and Washington. This presupposes constructive use of opportunities provided by bilateral cooperation in areas that meet our national interests, firm defense of Russian views when cooperation is unrealistic for some reason, and not backsliding into a confrontational stance with the United States. This is the key in which the Russian leadership intends to work with the new U.S. administration.

Asia and the Pacific Basin

Russia interests in Asia are quite varied, but all are extremely important. Involvement in European affairs as well as in Asian affairs is not just a unique geopolitical characteristic of the Russian state; it is also undeniably an asset. The dialectical unity and interconnectedness—rather than opposition—of the Euro-Atlantic and Asian-Pacific dimensions is the essence of Russia's foreign policy at the global level, as well as at the regional level.

The significant attention that Russia pays to Asia is not just dictated by the fact that two-thirds of Russia's territory lies on that continent. Asia is where the interests of the powers with the greatest nuclear potentials, most powerful militaries, and greatest economies intersect. The way in which international relations develop in this part of the world is a good indication of the path that will be chosen for harmonizing the legal interests of all peoples inhabiting the Asian continent, and to a larger degree, what the overall political climate of the planet will be and what its face will look like in the coming century.

With more than half the world's population, Asia today is a powerful center of global economic and technological development and the gathering place for the greatest financial resources in the world. The integration that is occurring in the Asian economy today will have consequences that reach far beyond the region's boundaries. At the threshold of the millennium, the far-flung Asian region has come through a formative period in all areas: economically, politically, militarily, socially, and culturally. This developmental stage was contradictory, blending an urge toward cooperation and search for new forms of interaction with competition and the attempts of some to rush in and fill the power vacuum left after the end of the cold war.

Despite Asia's complexity, its defining characteristic during the final decade of the twentieth century was its political stability, stemming from a positive dynamic that emerged as a result of the end of the cold war. The overwhelming majority of Asian countries were quick to grasp the modern world's future trends, and chose in favor of development and economic growth within a stable democratic world order, based on equality and a balance of interests. As a result, Asia has achieved levels of economic integration unprecedented in its history. A high level of integration—both bilateral and multilateral—has also been achieved in the area of regional security and peacekeeping. In this, the political, economic, cultural, and historical diversity of the region helped determine the multilateral nature of relations and the particular balance that was achieved between various centers of power.

Still, it would be a mistake to suppose that Asia's movement toward multipolarity alone was sufficient to support reliable peace and security in the region. The diversity of the Asian continent also created conditions that preserved considerable "heat," primarily accumulated in the past, such as problems resulting from territorial division and border disputes. There still remains some mutual distrust, built up over years of alienation and magnified by several key events into a bitter historical legacy. Asia also feels the direct influence of the entire range of contradictory global processes, especially militarily and politically. This is most clearly observed in the area of strategic weapons and antimissile defense systems. In Asia, the problem of proliferation of weapons of mass destruction is critical. Also, the contemporary problems of terrorism, religious extremism, separatism, illegal trafficking in weapons and drugs, and transnational crime have reared their heads throughout the Asia-Pacific basin. The worsening of other global problems—depletion of natural resources, the struggle for raw materials and energy sources, unchecked population growth, the degradation of the biosphere— affects the region as well.

Russia's national interests dictate its Asian diplomacy, which at its most basic focuses on ensuring the security of Russia's borders and helping to create favorable conditions for economic and social growth in the nations that lie to the south and to the east of the Urals. The primary way Russia pursues these goals is through active participation in multilateral and bilateral international efforts to support peace and military and political stability in the region, as well as by forming a regional security association based less on balances of power than on common interests and economic interdependence. Second, Russia pursues these goals by becoming more deeply involved in the inexorable processes of regional political and economic integration, and by intensively seeking new forms of mutually beneficial cooperation with Asian states. Russia's partners understand this perseverance, and we are seen as a natural participant in regional processes.

In recent years, Russian foreign policy with regard to Asia underwent a decisive turn, and the new direction will continue into the future. Proof of this is the continued development of bilateral relations with the region's leading states and active participation in regional integrating mechanisms, especially in the Pacific Basin.

Russia's relations with its largest neighbor, China, represent one of Russian foreign policy's strategic directions. For several years, Russian-Chinese political dialogue has been exceptionally intense and rich. The primary goal of Russian-Chinese relations was formulated in Moscow in the bilateral Joint Declaration on a Multipolar World and the Establishment of a New International Order (April 1997). The declaration established a "partnership based on equality and mutual trust for the purpose of strategic interaction in the twenty-first century."[28] It has already become a weighty factor in preserving global stability, which was made clearly apparent during the summer 2000 visit of President Putin to Beijing. During the visit of Jiang Zemin, president of the People's Republic of China, to Moscow the following summer, the two leaders signed a wide-scale Treaty for Good-Neighborliness, Friendship, and Cooperation, which laid out the principles for intergovernmental relations far into the future.[29] Acting as an independent pole in today's world, Moscow and Beijing intend to work together to make sure the new world order that is taking shape is as fair and as democratic as possible. The similarity of Russia's and China's basic positions is evident in their policies toward Asia. Both countries feel it is a priority to ensure security in the region, to create the conditions needed to bring about all-encompassing multilateral political cooperation, which would surely protect the interests of all nations in the region.

The groundwork is being laid for a reliable material base for trade and economic partnerships. The driving force for this cooperation can and should be provided by large-scale joint projects. There is huge potential for joint work in energy (including nuclear energy), the construction of fuel processing and transportation infrastructures, manufacturing, scientific research and development, and the implementation of new technology. Direct trade and economic ties at the regional level are becoming more and more significant.

The significance of the historic partnership between Russia and India cannot be overestimated. Cooperative efforts between our two countries have made an enormous contribution to stability in the region, and have done much to bring balance to the system of international relations as a whole. The future looks optimistic for the development of bilateral ties across the spectrum—from political and economic to military, technological, and humanitarian. This is firmly based on the coincidence of our two countries' national interests: we share a firm commitment to democratic values and we seek international and domestic stability as a prerequisite for accelerated economic growth. This shared position is what makes Moscow's and New Delhi's approaches to the basic issues of world politics so similar.

As an increasing priority in its relations with India, Russia would like to bring our political dialogue on trade and economic issues to a higher level. At present, trade and economic ties are falling far short of their potential. In this context, the outcome of President Putin's October 2000 visit to India is significant. An important document was signed during this visit—the Declaration on Strategic Partnership between Russia and India.[30] Likewise, the October 2001 visit of India's prime minister, Atal Behari Vajpayee, to Russia signifies the beginning of a new era in our bilateral relations.

Qualitative changes are taking place in our relations with Japan, where substantial progress has been made in recent years. Russian-Japanese summit meetings are now taking place on a regular schedule. The prime minister of Japan's visit to Russia in November 1998 was the first in over a quarter of a century. The main outcome of this trip was the adoption of the Moscow Declaration on building a creative long-term partnership between our two countries.[31] Russian-Japanese relations were advanced considerably and reinvigorated by President Putin's visit to Japan in September 2000. For the first time in the history of our two countries, the president of Russia and the prime minister of Japan issued a joint statement on cooperation between the two countries on international affairs. The statement included a declaration by Japan on the importance of Russia's entry into the WTO, and support from Russia of Japan's candidacy for UN Security Council membership. On the whole, 2000 was a "bumper crop" year for foreign policy. Nevertheless, there remains the unresolved issue of agreement on an internationally recognized Russia-Japan border in the Southern Kuril Islands. Obviously, this complex problem must be resolved in a mutually acceptable way, without damage to the sovereignty or territorial integrity of the Russian Federation. Any solution must be in accordance with national interests, must be based on existing realities, must have broad popular support, and must be constitutionally approved by both countries' highest lawmaking bodies.

In general, Russia is poised to enter into a wide range of long-term relations with Japan, including closer coordination in international affairs, trade and economic expansion, and greater cooperation in other areas.

Russia's policies toward the Korean peninsula are guided by the need to maintain balanced, open relations and partnerships with both Korean states. 2000 was a watershed in our relations with North Korea. The signing of a new full-scale interstate treaty between Russia and North Korea put an end to ten years of chilly relations between the two countries. President Putin made the first visit to North Korea in the history of our bilateral relations, and North Korean head of state Kim Jong-il made a reciprocal visit to Russia. 2001 saw a summit meeting in South Korea that strengthened forward-looking developments in Russian–South Korean cooperation. This balanced approach allows Russia to play a constructive role, facilitating progress in reconciliation between North and South Korea and strengthening security and stability on the peninsula. The first inter-Korea summit, held in Pyongyang in mid-June 2000, has opened up the possibility of peaceful coexistence on the Korean peninsula. More active interaction between Russia and the two Korean governments is extremely important for more productive dialogue on standardizing Korean relations with the United States, China, and Japan.

The geography of South and Southwest Asia, and its growing economic, military, and political potential, leave no alternative to the constant cultivation of broad cooperative efforts between Russia and the countries in this region. The primary goal is to transform this part of the Asian continent from an arena of confrontation into a zone of predictability and stability, a transformation that will improve conditions on Russia's southern and eastern borders.

Recognizing the key role played by India and Pakistan in the South Asian subcontinent, Russia advocates normalized relations, continued bilateral dialogue, and the development of measures of trust between these two countries. This is imperative with regard to the historic disagreement over Kashmir, which must be resolved peacefully, on the basis of the 1972 Shimla Agreement and the 1999 Lahore Declaration. Russia has consistently sought and continues to insist that both India and

Pakistan sign the Comprehensive Test Ban Treaty and that they join the Non-Proliferation Treaty. Despite the many nuclear tests conducted by India and Pakistan in May 1998, Russia does not consider these countries to be nuclear powers, and therefore calls for them to join the CTBT in this capacity. The rest of the "nuclear five" hold this position as well. The Russian leadership has unequivocally stated that nuclear testing by India and Pakistan cannot have a positive effect on the situation in South Asia. However, Russia is not in favor of implementing sanctions against India or Pakistan for this reason, because such action is not justified either by international law or on humanitarian grounds.

The prolonged conflict in Afghanistan adds a significant international dimension to the situation in south-central Asia. Ravaged for many years by civil war, this country has become the primary international launching ground for the expansion of terrorism and religious extremism. This poses a serious threat to Russia's security and to that of its allies in the region, and also to many other states. We warned the international community several times about massive efforts that were under way in Taliban-controlled territory to train and prepare fighters who had come from the North Caucasus region of Russia and from other states in Central Asia, the Arab world, and elsewhere. Financed heavily by flourishing Afghan narco-business and other illegal activities, the terrorists began to gain strength and resources. The tragic events of September 11 were the monstrous fulfillment of their criminal plans. Russia has repeatedly called for the mobilization of international efforts for decisive and clearly coordinated action against the threats coming out of Afghanistan. We actively support the antiterrorist coalition that has entered into battle with the Taliban and other terrorist groups. Obviously, the return of Afghanistan to the international family will be a lengthy process and will demand consistent coordinated action by the world community. The UN must play a central role in regulating the situation inside Afghanistan. For its part, Moscow is prepared to continue in every possible way to help restore peace to Afghanistan and to overcome the destructive consequences of infighting between factions.

Iran is an important partner of Russia in Central Asia. Teheran's influence and authority is widely accepted in the Islamic world. The Russian-Iranian relationship traditionally has been characterized by goodwill and openness. Moreover, both states share very similar approaches to solving many regional and global problems. The successful development of cooperative efforts has become an important positive factor in regional politics. A sign of this was the regulation of the situation in Tajikistan, in which both Moscow and Teheran made important contributions to the conclusion of the inter-Tajik agreements ending the civil war and acted as guarantors of their implementation. Their shared positions also guide Iran and Russia in regard to the situation in Afghanistan today.

Successful Russian-Iranian political cooperation is strengthened by serious opportunities for mutually beneficial cooperation in trade and economics. Currently, plans are under way for a variety of large bilateral projects in the oil and gas industries, in energy, in aviation construction, and in transportation.

In recent years, the Asia-Pacific Basin region has seen a significant increase in integration and cooperation, in trade and economics as well as politically. The primary organization for economic integration in the region—the Asia-Pacific Economic Cooperation (APEC) forum—has seen increased development. Other organizations—like ASEAN's institute for political dialogue, the ASEAN Regional Forum (ARF)—are gaining strength, as is the Asia-Europe Meeting, a mechanism for regular summit meetings between the two regions. Under discussion is the formation of a pan-Asian system for dialogue, reaching from the Middle East to the Russian Far East, and based on an initiative of the Kazakhstan Conference for Cooperation and Trust-Building Measures in Central Asia. The role of many subregional organizations is growing as well: the Shanghai Cooperation Organization (joining Kazakhstan, China, the Kyrgyz Republic, Russia, Tajikistan, and Uzbekistan); ASEAN+3 (a mechanism for consultation, including China, Japan, and South Korea); the Indian Ocean Rim Association for Regional Cooperation (IOR-ARC); and other organizations for economic cooperation involving Bangladesh, India, Myanmar, Sri Lanka, and Thailand, to name but a few.

Russia actively seeks to expand ties and create new infrastructures for cooperation with the Association of Southeast Asian Nations (ASEAN). Today, this influential body unites all nations in the wide area of Southeast Asia. At the center of the region's cooperative security efforts is the ASEAN Regional Forum, in which all the leading states participate, including China, Japan, and India, as well as the United States and the European Union.

Within the ARF framework, Russia fully participates in discussions on the region's current problems and issues, bringing to bear its multilateral diplomatic resources. It is in Russia's interest to help create a collective security system in Asia. Russia advocates a more high-profile role for the ARF as the key regional institution for dialogue on policy and security and values the concept and implementation work done by ARF members on preventative diplomacy for the Asia-Pacific region. These efforts might effectively be organized by the "Pacific Accord," a Russia-initiated draft declaration on the guiding principles for relations in the Asia-Pacific region that could act as a kind of code of conduct. Parallel to this initiative are other ARF efforts to implement new measures for trust in the military and political spheres, and to expand dialogue into other areas where cooperation could enhance regional security.

Integration of the Asia-Pacific region's economic system is one of Russia's top policy priorities. Policy development in this area is guided by our need to effectively use the economic potential of Russia's eastern regions, to stimulate and support Russia's industrial sector, to improve the health of our credit and financial systems, to create a favorable climate for investment, and to attract foreign capital. Russia has resources and assets to share with its partners in the region. There are already approximately 400 businesses operating in the Asia-Pacific region that have received Russian capital, and more than 1,000 joint ventures have been registered to do business in the Russian Far East. Russia has everything needed to create a transportation corridor that would bring the Euro-Atlantic and Asia-Pacific regions significantly closer together. Russia also has the capability to provide for the growing energy needs of the region. Indeed, the energy potential of Siberia and the Far East make the establishment of a unified Europe-Asia energy system a very real possibility in the coming century.

During the past decade, Russia joined most of the regional and subregional organizations in Asia and the Pacific Basin and expressed its full readiness to seek Asian-Pacific economic integration. In November 1998, Russia was accepted into the largest body working toward integration, the twenty-one-country Asia-Pacific Economic Cooperation forum.

The APEC forum is the engine that drives the region's integration process. Its members account for some 60 percent of the world's GNP and approximately half of the volume of international trade. By joining

APEC, Russia demonstrates its strategic commitment to economic integration with the Asia-Pacific region and displays its intent to fully exploit the benefits of an international division of labor. The most promising areas for Russia's participation in regional APEC projects include science and technology, energy, transportation, marine resources, environmental protection, and tourism. Russia's active participation in the trade and investment liberalization promoted by APEC in the region is very much connected with Russia's prospective membership in the WTO. In preparation for the November 2000 APEC summit in Brunei, President Putin remarked, "Russia's full participation in economic cooperative processes in the Asia-Pacific area is natural and inevitable. . . . Today, we see the full range of opportunities for cooperation: in energy, on economic issues, in the development of the continental shelf, the development of transportation links, and in the implementation of specific economic and investment projects."[32]

An excellent example of well-coordinated multilateral cooperation on security issues in which Russia participates is the Shanghai Five Process. The agreements reached by its members on confidence-building measures and the demilitarization of shared borders do much to strengthen stability in the entire region. Significantly, cooperation of this kind is transparent and is not directed by the group against other countries. Motivated by a desire to expand the areas of their cooperation, the group adopted a resolution at their June 15, 2001, meeting in Shanghai to become the Shanghai Cooperation Organization, composed of Russia, Kazakhstan, China, Kyrgyzstan, Tajikistan, and Uzbekistan. The group's primary goals are improved trust, friendship, and openness between its members; increased cooperation in a broad range of areas; deeper cooperation on peace issues; and the formation of an international political and economic order, based on democracy and justice. The big picture shows the group forging a new culture of intergovernmental communication, a culture of coordinated development amid the complexities of the twenty-first century.[33]

Asia is moving up on Russia's scale of foreign policy priorities. This is an objective process, related chiefly to Asia's growing role in the global economy and world development. The words spoken by Indian politician and statesman Jawaharlal Nehru over half a century ago are more relevant today than ever before. He said that without the energetic involvement of Asia in the process, peace and stability would be unattainable on our planet. Russia is optimistic about the Asia-Pacific region's future. It is within the region's power to harmonize relations between states and to build consensus on transforming the region into a peaceful and prosperous cooperative association.

The Middle East and North Africa

Russia has always viewed the Middle East in a special light, as the birthplace of three world religions. Unfortunately, during the past ten years this region has been wracked with conflicts that periodically escalate into military confrontations that resonate around the globe. In addition, the region is significant as one of the world's primary sources of oil and other fossil fuels. Russia's active participation in Middle East affairs is naturally a product of our geopolitical location. In this era of globalization, the tension within the Middle East has an increased impact on security and stability in a wide area immediately adjoining Russia's southern border, a region that Russia would like to see become a zone of peace and stability.

Russia's relations with the Middle East and North Africa go back for a millennium. Our potential for cooperation is built on this long history—dating back to the first visits of Russian pilgrims to the Holy Land and the construction of Russian schools and hospitals in Palestine and Syria in the last century. In the modern era, Russia has trained a veritable army of highly qualified specialists from the region, equipped large industrial installations, and helped to develop the national economies of several Arab nations. We also had a hand in one of the wonders of engineering of the twentieth century: the Aswan High Dam and hydroelectric complex.

Russia's approach to the Middle East has undergone substantial change over the last ten years. The time has long passed when this region was a focal point for confrontation between the superpowers. Through painstaking diplomatic efforts, Russia has reached a point where it is able to sustain and develop relations both with Israel and with all the Arab nations. This has not been easy. For many reasons, both objective and subjective, traditionally robust relations between Russia and the Arab world were sharply curtailed in the early 1990s. As a result, our political influence and our trade and economic involvement in the region suffered. Russia's place in Arab markets was gradually taken over by other states. We were faced with the urgent challenge of restoring multilateral cooperative efforts with former partners in the Middle East and North Africa, and we have largely been successful. Today Russia engages in intense political dialogue with the nations of this region. In 2000–01, the Russian minister of foreign affairs made official visits to Egypt, Israel, the Palestinian National Authority, Syria, Lebanon, Jordan, Kuwait, Iraq, and Saudi Arabia. During the first half of 2001 alone, Russia was visited by the presidents of Israel and Egypt, the leader of Palestine, the vice president of Iraq, and the foreign affairs ministers of Syria, Israel, and Yemen. Russia is also cultivating relations with the nations of North Africa that are part of the important Mediterranean region. The Russian minister of foreign affairs has made official visits to Algeria and Libya, and Moscow has received the president of Algeria and the foreign affairs minister of Tunisia.

Russia's efforts to actively engage nations in the region have yielded tangible results in the area of economics. Our volume of trade with the Middle East and North Africa is growing, comprising approximately $5 billion in 2000. We continue to find more and more ways to work together: one example is Egypt's investment in the Russian aviation industry.[34]

Russia's balanced policies allow us to play a prominent role in efforts to ease the conflict in this region. Largely as a result of our country's efforts, Libya has been drawn out of its international isolation. As cosponsor of the Middle East peace process—and without Russia's participation, the process would surely never have gotten off the ground in Madrid—Russia does a great deal toward the regulation of the Arab-Israeli situation. Russia seeks to bring stability and inclusiveness to this process, as outlined in resolutions 242 and 338 of the UN Security Council, and based on the principle of "land for peace." As cosponsor, Russia vigorously encourages the Arabs and Israelis to seek and to strictly observe clear, mutually acceptable agreements, and not to make unrealistic demands or take any unilateral actions. Moscow fully supports the unquestionable right of the Palestinians to have their own sovereign nation, and the establishment of this nation through a peaceful process.

Russia sees enormous significance in the outcome of the permanent status negotiations and in the fair and mutually acceptable resolution to the issue of Palestinian refugees. Any agreements reached must adequately address Israel's security concerns related to the formation of an independent Palestinian state. Russia favors broad and coordinated international efforts to advance the peace process. Experience shows that the monopolization of mediation efforts by a single state, no matter how much influence it may wield vis-à-vis the conflict's participants, is ultimately counterproductive. The worsening of the Middle East situation in fall 2000 demonstrated again the need not only for U.S. efforts, but also for Russia, the European Union, leading Arab nations—especially Egypt and Jordan—and the United Nations to bring their resources to bear.

Russia maintains close contact with others who have been drawn into the conflict, with the goal of developing vigorous measures to bring about an end to Israeli-Palestinian fighting, and to set in motion a stable negotiation process. I am convinced that despite the drama unfolding in the Palestinian territories, there is no sensible alternative to continuing the peace process.

Events of 2000–01 in the region confirmed that stable regulation of the Middle East conflict cannot be attained unless every avenue of the peace process is explored. For this reason, Russia is paying constant attention to the Israel-Syria and Israel-Lebanon negotiating tracks. After Israel's withdrawal of troops from southern Lebanon in May, 2000, as stipulated by UN Security Council resolution 425, Russia actively sought to maintain the positive momentum of this development and not to allow any new or further complications to arise on the Lebanese-Israeli border. Russian diplomacy works persistently to restore the Israel-Syria dialogue; we see this as key to the future of the peace process in the region.

Russian diplomacy is playing a leadership role through initiatives to transform the Persian Gulf into a zone of peace, security, and goodwill, in hopes of avoiding a repeat of the wars and conflicts that have occurred in this strategically important region of the world. Ideas advanced by

Russia include the implementation of a wide array of political, military, economic, and humanitarian measures and the establishment of a system of agreements with corresponding international guarantees.

Key elements of any postcrisis reconstruction in the Persian Gulf, in Russia's view, would include regulation of the situation concerning Iraq and normalization of relations between all the nations in this region. It is imperative to reduce the threat of military action, to stop the arms race, to reduce the foreign military presence, and to develop confidence-building measures and measures that restore wide regional cooperation. An integral feature of all these efforts should be the establishment of a zone free of weapons of mass destruction. The regulation process would be given more teeth by the institution of a regional organization to monitor peace and stability in the area. In addition to Persian Gulf states, this organization should include the UN Security Council's permanent members and other interested parties.

Russia also plays an important role in the regulation of the Iraqi problem, leading international efforts to break the impasse through political means. Acting within the UN and through contacts with other UN Security Council permanent members, Russia seeks to accelerate the lifting of sanctions against Iraq, based on its compliance with the appropriate Security Council resolutions. We believe that the occasional air strikes carried out against Iraqi territory by the United States and Britain are illegal, and it is obvious that such actions are counterproductive. These air strikes were directly responsible for the withdrawal of UN weapons inspectors from Iraq in December 1998 and for the cessation of all international monitoring efforts. Despite these events, Russia is actively working to establish a dialogue between Baghdad and the UN, an important element in finding solutions to the problem. Consistent diplomatic efforts by Russia to ease the predicament of the Iraqi population helped make possible the UN "oil for food" humanitarian aid program, in which Russian companies took an active part. We are also laying the groundwork necessary to resume trade and economic cooperation with Iraq, once the sanctions are lifted.

Events in the Middle East—a region where the potential for violent conflict has been accumulating for decades—demonstrate that the management of complex regional problems on the basis of equal security for all states is an indispensable condition for the achievement of international stability and the development of a new world order.

Latin America and the Caribbean

Relations with Latin America and the nations of the Caribbean basin make up an independent and very promising area in Russia's multifaceted foreign policy. Many factors have combined to bring Russia into ever-closer contact with the nations of this region.

Russia has old historical ties to Latin America. Diplomatic relations were established with Brazil in 1828, with Argentina in 1885, and with Mexico in 1890. The history of Russian–Latin American relations contains many instances of sincere mutual compassion, of brilliant ethnic and cultural exchange, and of mutual solidarity and support, even during the cold war, with its myriad ideological obstacles.

Accelerated economic development and integration in Latin America during the 1990s transformed this region into one of the most important independent poles in the multipolar world now taking shape. The role of Latin American countries in international affairs has grown substantially, since they do not limit their foreign policy to regional issues and have begun to take a more active role in addressing global policy issues. Objectively, Latin American diplomacy resembles that of Russia in several key aspects. Latin America and Russia share an interest in strengthening multilateral diplomacy and in increasing the role of the UN in the world, and both have a strong tradition of adhering to international law. Russia cannot help but respect the foreign policy orientation of Latin America, which was summed up neatly in the nineteenth century by the Mexican national hero Benito Juárez (1806–72), who said, "respect for the rights of others is Peace."

Economically, Latin America was one of the most dynamically developing regions of the world in the 1990s. By many indicators, several Latin American nations very nearly pulled abreast of the industrially developed nations. Although the global financial crisis deeply affected the Latin American economy, this growing market holds much promise for Russian business and industry, especially for some high-technology projects (including in the fields of aircraft technology, automobile production, and satellite launches).

Russia is interested in Latin America's success in creating effective integrated institutions for cooperative work within regional organizations, like the Organization of American States, the Latin American Integration Association, the Rio Group on Poverty Statistics, the Southern Cone Common Market (Mercosur), the Andean Development Corporation, and others.

We are also very interested in parallels between Russia's very recent history and the experience of many Latin American countries undergoing their own serious democratic transformation and economic reform. The collapse of military dictatorships throughout the region means that Latin America has gained valuable insight into building and strengthening democratic institutions of power. Latin America is also a unique proving ground for market transformation, and Russia's social and political leaders are keeping a close eye on the results, hoping to learn from what has worked successfully, as well as to avoid pitfalls in the process of transition.

The final decade of the twentieth century brought enormous changes in Russian–Latin American relations. Despite the complexity and difficulty of this transformational process, the end result is undeniably positive. Russia's diplomatic presence now has a significantly greater geographical distribution. Relations have been established with many nations that were previously cut off from Russia. Today, the Russian Federation maintains diplomatic relations with twenty-eight of the thirty-three sovereign nations of Latin America—the only exceptions being some of the Caribbean island states. Russia has many new opportunities for developing multilateral contacts in the area, aided by the establishment of ties to regional organizations and integrated associations, and by being granted permanent observer status to the Organization of American States in 1992. Russian–Latin American relations have taken a more vigorous turn since the mid-1990s. Important milestones were visits of then Russian minister of foreign affairs Yevgeny Primakov to Mexico, Venezuela, Brazil, Argentina, Colombia, Costa Rica, and Cuba in May 1996 and November 1997. Visits to Moscow were made by the president of Argentina in 1998, by the vice president of Brazil in 2000, by the president of Venezuela in 2001, and by the heads of many of Latin America's foreign policy agencies. Russian–Latin American cooperation was significantly advanced when President Vladimir Putin made the first top-level visit in Russian history to Latin America by visiting Cuba in December 2000. During the September 2000 Millennium Summit in New York and the November 2000 APEC forum in Brunei, President Putin also met, for the first time, with the leaders of Mexico, Venezuela, and Chile.

The juridical base of Russian–Latin American relations has been substantially renewed and expanded. From 1992 to 2000, more than 140 bilateral documents were signed, among them "new generation" treaties and declarations laying the foundations for relations and principles of cooperation. The agreements covered trade and economic, scientific, and technological cooperation, as well as the encouragement and mutual protection of investments, cultural exchanges, space exploration and development, efforts to fight narco-business, and so on.[35]

Russia's political contacts with the Rio Group have been qualitatively enhanced. Since 1997, foreign ministers' meetings have been regularly held at UN General Assembly sessions in New York, and an ongoing calendar and substantive agenda for Russia's dialogue with this association have been established. Russian diplomacy has established contacts with the Ibero-American Forum, which unites the Spanish- and Portuguese-speaking countries of Europe and the Americas. Initial steps have been taken to foster direct dialogue and contacts with Mercosur and with the Andean Community. Russia has also been granted permanent observer status at the Association of Caribbean States (ACS).

Practical efforts by Russian diplomacy in Latin American presently focus on expanding as much as possible the scope of our countries' cooperation in international affairs, by stepping up mutually beneficial economic cooperation and by strengthening our diverse range of cultural, educational, and personal ties.

Russia regards the Latin American states as natural partners in the international arena, above all in resolving the key issue of forming an equitable and stable world order, based on the supremacy of international law and on strong democratic, multilateral institutions for managing global interaction. We are united by our shared commitment to preserving the central role of the UN and the Security Council's primary responsibility for maintaining international peace and security. We also share an interest in promoting strategic stability and in searching for collective answers to new threats and challenges. Russia has greatly appreciated the support shown by Latin American and Caribbean countries in the UN General Assembly, when sixteen Latin American and Caribbean states voted to support Russia's draft resolution in favor of preserving the 1972 ABM Treaty as the cornerstone of strategic stability in the world. These supporters included not only prominent members of the Latin American community, such as Mexico and Colombia, but also such countries as Honduras, Panama, and Caribbean island states.

Latin America is gradually forming its own concept of regional security. One of the main foundations of this concept is the juridical confirmation of the region's nuclear-free status in accordance with the Treaty of Tlatelolco,[36] which has been in force for three decades. The position of leading Latin American countries—Brazil and Argentina, in particular—on this matter undoubtedly represents a substantial contribution to resolving the global problem of strengthening nonproliferation regimes for nuclear weapons. The region's countries have also become more active in other areas of the disarmament process, particularly in efforts to declare the Western Hemisphere a zone free from land mines and to adopt a regional convention prohibiting the illegal production and sale of firearms.

Peace making is an important area of cooperation between Russia and Latin America. The region's nations have gained useful experience in the independent political settlement of many domestic and regional conflicts. Russia has always supported these efforts, having played a constructive role in resolving a number of protracted conflicts in Central America (Nicaragua, El Salvador, and Guatemala). We have also reiterated our readiness to provide political assistance in the peaceful resolution of Colombia's complicated internal situation, where the problem of leftist insurgents is intertwined with the fight against narco-business and with efforts to protect human rights. Russia recognizes Latin America's substantial contributions to developing political principles and practical guidelines for the fight against the production and sale of illegal drugs, and to the preparation of the special 1998 UN General Assembly session on illegal drugs. Cooperation between Russia and Latin America in this area is gaining momentum. Eight bilateral agreements have been signed with Latin American states on cooperation in this field that enable law enforcement agencies to combine efforts in the fight against Latin American drug dealers and Russian criminal groups.

The unresolved issue of Cuba remains a serious political problem in the Western Hemisphere. The forty-year blockade and trade and economic embargo by the United States against Cuba are unacceptable, both to Russia and to the majority of other countries. This policy is an obvious anachronism that meets no one's interests, including those of the United States itself. Extraterritorial attempts to enact the Helms-Burton Act and U.S. legislation to increase restrictions on the relations that third-party sovereign states can have with Cuba have been rejected all over the world. Russia advocates a full normalization of the Cuban situation. This means lifting the embargo and reintegrating the country into regional cooperative institutions. Russia respects the political choice of the Cuban people and remains true to its traditional view that human rights should serve to unite nations and peoples, not to separate them.

The official visit of President Putin to Cuba in December 2000 demonstrated that the Russian and Cuban leaderships both possess the political will to reinvigorate relations, to remove the barriers to bilateral ties that arose in the early 1990s, and to define the future of economic cooperation between the two states. The talks in Havana produced an important basic agreement: that Russia and Cuba intend to continue the development of active cooperation between themselves.[37] This is a high-level agreement supported by the feelings of friendship and understanding that exist between our countries and peoples. Of course, such ties must be based on the realities of both countries, on the principles of international law and mutual benefit, and on the rules of international competition.

Trade and economic cooperation between Russia and Latin America is very important to us. After a period of some decline, Russian trade with Latin American countries began to develop again in recent years: its volume reached nearly $3 billion in 1999. Food purchases by private Russian companies account for a substantial portion of this trade. Russia has become one of the main importers of Brazilian, Colombian, and

Chilean instant coffee. Other trade is also being developed successfully: Russia imports vegetable oil, cocoa, tropical fruits and fruit concentrates, nonalcoholic beverages, and flowers. Our principal trading partners in the region are Cuba, Brazil, Ecuador, Argentina, and Chile. Individual cooperative investment projects are being implemented with Argentina, Brazil, Cuba, Nicaragua, and Ecuador. Despite these achievements, the present scope of trade and economic ties still falls short of potential. This is especially true since the Russian and Latin American economies are complementary in many areas, which makes them potential partners rather than competitors in world markets.

Several obstacles hinder the development of trade and economic ties between us. One objective difficulty is our geographic separation. Another negative factor is the generalized financial and economic crisis that materialized in 1998 in both Russia and Latin America. Russian exports are still subject to unfair competition. We have, however, managed to achieve some improvement in this area, in particular through involvement with the Andean Community. And yet the underlying problem lies elsewhere: our cooperative efforts are obviously insufficiently diversified, and there exists no effective financial mechanism for the mutual guarantee of investments. Russia will assist—at the highest political level—in finding ways to resolve these issues. As a practical step, intergovernmental commissions on trade and economic, scientific, and technological cooperation with Cuba, Mexico, Argentina, and Colombia have been reestablished. Moreover, the creation of the High-Level Commission on Cooperation with Brazil effectively gives this country the same status as Russia's most important partners, since similar commissions exist only for such countries as France, China, and Ukraine. In 1998 we established the National Committee for Economic Cooperation with Latin American States, which works to foster business ties and information exchange, to study growth areas for cooperation, and in general, to create a favorable climate for Russian–Latin American business relations.

Having come through a complicated and occasionally painful stage of transformation during the early 1990s, Russian–Latin American relations are now reaching a qualitatively new level of development, founded on constructive cooperation and mutual benefit.

Africa

Russia is open to the development of friendly relations and mutually beneficial cooperation with African nations. Historically, there is fertile ground for this: during the second half of the twentieth century, and despite the costs of maintaining the cold war and a confrontational ideology, Russia never failed to support Africa in its fight for political independence and stable economic development.

Today, Russia sees the African states as our partners in the work of forming a new and democratic world order. Obviously, Africa's interests require a system of international relations that gives priority to equitable multilateral mechanisms for resolving global issues, especially in trade and economics. Russia and Africa are united by a common interest in defending the foundation and principles of international law and in blocking efforts to use force in the settlement of disputes.

Based on this position, Russia is prepared to continue active dialogue with African states, whether bilaterally, at the UN, or in conjunction with the Non-Aligned Movement, the African Union, or other regional bodies. Just as important as international issues as a topic for dialogue is the regulation of conflict situations on the African continent. Russia has played, and will continue to play, a constructive role in efforts to restore peace in Angola and to regulate the conflict between Ethiopia and Eritrea, among others. Russian diplomacy facilitates Africa's peacemaking potential and the formation of a basis for collective security on the continent. We also continue to foster cooperation with pan-African, regional, and subregional organizations: the Organization for African Unity (OAU), the Southern Africa Development Community (SADC), the Economic Community of West African States (ECOWAS), and the Inter-Governmental Authority for Development (IGAD).

Russia applauds the success achieved in peace-making and integration efforts by the OAU, by subregional bodies, and through the initiatives in this area promoted by certain African heads of state. Russia stands ready for participation in future multilateral and bilateral efforts to ensure peace and stability in this region.

One of the most pressing issues in Russia's African policy is the need to identify the optimal model for developing trade and economic ties with Africa, a model that corresponds to the realistic capabilities of our country. Because of the fundamental socioeconomic changes that have occurred within Russia, any effective model must prominently feature participation by Russian and African private enterprise. Despite a substantial reduction in Russia's trade volume with Africa—by 1994 it had fallen to $740 million, as compared with $2.7 billion just before the collapse of the Soviet Union—there definitely exist opportunities for mutually beneficial trade. Russia is prepared to offer to its African partners modern Russian technology of all kinds: industrial, agricultural, housing construction, medical, and others. Still, the complex issue of Russia's foreign trade imbalance with African countries remains serious. The imbalance is in Russia's favor: in 1998 our exports to Africa totaled $1 billion, while our imports from Africa stood at only $427.8 million.

Russia advocates a comprehensive approach to solving Africa's serious problems and supports organized joint study of every key aspect—social, humanitarian, economic, political, and military—to ensure stable development for all African states.

4

NEW HORIZONS

Foreign Policy and the Economy

The central goal of Russian foreign policy was and remains creating the optimal external conditions for continued domestic transformation that strengthens the government, improves the economy, and increases the well-being of Russian citizens. The role of "economic diplomacy" in Russian foreign policy is continually increasing. This reflects a global trend: economic factors exert an increasingly substantial influence on states' foreign policy and on the development of international relations at regional and global levels.

Specifically, this translates into the ever wider and more active use of Russia's foreign policy and diplomatic tools to help achieve goals such as

—economic stabilization and stable economic growth

—the full-scale integration of Russia into the world economy, which includes participation in international economic organizations

—the entry of Russian enterprises into foreign markets

—the creation of conditions necessary for equitable and nondiscriminatory trade with foreign partners

—ensuring a favorable climate to attract foreign investment and relieve our foreign debt

These goals require increasingly close coordination between the state's foreign policy activities and its policies relating to the domestic economy and to external economic activity. The mutual interdependence here is obvious: foreign policy can be effective only if supported by all the resources of the state and society. In our globalized society, foreign policy can and should serve as a powerful means of leveraging this array of resources for maximum effect, through well-organized programs of international cooperation that are coordinated with a state's national interests. In other words, foreign policy today, as never before, should be viewed as an integral part of a state's plan for strategic development.

In this vein, President Putin has proposed a program that spells out the opportunities for using foreign policy to achieve economic growth. The program outlines measures that multilaterally strengthen and improve Russian democracy and, more important, that solidify the government's role as we continue to build a socially oriented market economy. One of the program's main elements is the use of concrete actions that strengthen our economy's material base as a supplement to macroeconomic stability. Specifically, it calls for a more genuinely competitive economic environment, for the establishment of universal rules of the game that are stable and transparent and apply to all market entrants, for strengthening market institutions, and for vigorously fighting corruption. Each of these issues is affected by an important external factor: efforts to further integrate Russia into the global economic system and into the network of international economic organizations necessitate corresponding measures to bring our economy in line with the norms and standards required for all participants in the global economic system.

In actuality, Russian diplomatic activity relating to external economics can be broken down into the following main areas. First, Russia is highly interested in the specific nature of the international economic system into which it is trying to integrate. For this reason, we have a vested interest in the collective search for ways to manage globalization and must be involved in decisions that guide long-range economic trends and shape global economic processes.

In recent years, the primary channel through which our country could participate in discussions and development work of this nature was via the framework of the G-8. At first, Russia participated in these leadership meetings of the seven major industrially developed countries only as a partner in political dialogue. Today, Russia participates in conferences with representatives of these states at all levels and across virtually the entire range of issues under discussion: from world economics to various aspects of cooperation in resolving global questions that touch on the areas of sociology, ecology, and law, among other areas.

Another area where Russia's interests intersect with the world economy is our emphasis on increasing interaction with international economic organizations. On the external economic front, an important immediate goal for Russia is membership in the World Trade Organization, which was established January 1, 1995. The WTO's primary mission is to facilitate the gradual liberalization of world trade by eliminating various nontariff barriers and other obstacles to international trade in goods and services.

Russian diplomacy is supportive of the negotiation process required for Russia's entry into the WTO. The issue of our WTO membership is on the agenda for meetings between the highest level of Russian leadership and leaders of the countries with which we do the most trade: the United States, Germany, France, Canada, Japan, and others. At the June 1999 G-8 summit in Köln, the leading industrialized countries voiced their support for Russia on this issue. The leadership and representatives of Russia's Foreign Affairs Ministry are in ongoing discussions on the general political implications of Russia joining the WTO with regional organizations in Europe and the Asia-Pacific area. At a bilateral level, this issue is addressed by our representatives within the framework of intergovernmental commissions on trade and economic cooperation, on official visits at all levels, and in consultations with the foreign affairs departments of our partners.

In negotiations on this issue, Russia makes it clear that we seek to join the WTO to help improve our own domestic economy, to eliminate trade discrimination, and to create more favorable conditions for Russian exports. Russia's entry into the WTO would be standard and like that of any other member-state, with no special restrictions. That said, it is important for us that all other WTO members acknowledge the unique circumstances of Russia's economy related to our large-scale reforms, and that we be granted, if need be, an adjustment period to fully adapt to certain WTO requirements.

A third important area of diplomatic effort relating to external economics is our support for trade, economic, and investment cooperation between Russia and foreign partners, both in the context of large integrated organizations and on a bilateral basis. Here, a priority for Russia is developing cooperation within the CIS, on multiple levels and at different rates. After an abrupt drop during the first half of the 1990s, there has been a moderate increase in economic ties between Russia and CIS states in recent years. However, the level of this activity is still not where it should be. Increased economic cooperation and further integration within the CIS are only possible if based on market relations, and with greater involvement of industrial finance and banking capital. Here, too, it is obvious that at the present stage a stable increase in trade and economic cooperation is only possible with narrowly focused state support and regulation. This combination of market mechanics and state regulation makes possible the optimal marriage between solutions to our immediate problems and vision toward mid- and long-range opportunities, and an organic whole interconnecting the economic, social, and political aspects of cooperation.

Russia sees much promise in the upswing in broad cooperative efforts between Russia and the European Union. The EU is the largest integrated economic union in the world and has emerged as Russia's leading trade partner (34 percent of Russian foreign trade is conducted with the EU, as compared with 22 percent with the CIS and 3 to 6 percent with China, the United States, and Japan).[1] In turn, Russia ranks fifth in volume of imports into the EU and sixth in volume of exports received from the EU. Russia concentrates most of its foreign assets in the EU, and has historically maintained a positive trade balance with the European Union.

Trade and economic cooperation between Russia and the EU is made easier by our close geographic proximity, by the fact that our economies and infrastructures complement each other, by a shared juridical base for interaction, and by a long history of previous business and trade. With its vast industrial, financial, trade, investment, and scientific resources, the European Union will play an increasingly strategic role in Russia's foreign dealings. It is the EU that provides a large and steady market for traditional Russian goods: gas, oil and petroleum products, coal, lumber, metal ore, fertilizer, chemicals, nuclear power cycle products, diamonds, and so on.

Russia's export profile does not coincide with the structure of the EU's overall imports, while Russia's imports from the EU do correspond to the EU's overall export profile. Industrial products predominate in both the EU's exports and its imports. This presents an opportunity for Russia to increase its industrial exports to the European Union as we increase the competitiveness of Russia's industrial output. Moreover, the EU's low import duties are also an important factor in improving Russia's export profile.

Another important circumstance is that the European Union imports much of its energy and raw materials from Russia. In turn, Russia's foreign trade is primarily oriented toward the export of these goods and should remain so for the foreseeable future. Consequently, the European Union represents enormous market potential for Russia, which would be able to maintain a positive balance in its trade with the EU.

An important area for partnership with the European Union is cooperation in investment. The EU is the leading investor in Russia's economy and, despite difficulties and losses caused by the events of recent years, European investors have tended to stay involved in the Russian market. According to data from the Russian State Committee on Statistics, as of June 1, 1998, the total accumulated investment of European countries in Russia's economy was approximately $21.3 billion, more than 79 percent of Russia's total foreign investment. Foreign direct investment from European countries represented $5.34 billion, or 62 percent of all direct investment in the Russian economy. Cooperation with European firms and companies on effective investment projects in Russia is being carried out in the automotive, aerospace, and processed food industries, as well as in metallurgy, communication electronics, and other areas. European investors are also very active in oil and natural gas production.

Still, Russian-EU trade and economic cooperation is experiencing increasing difficulties that threaten to complicate further growth and development. The European Union continues to support discriminatory trade policies that restrict the import of some Russian goods. The Agreement on Partnership and Cooperation between Russia and the EU gave Russian goods and services more liberal access to EU markets, and tariff barriers to EU markets have been lowered for Russian exports.[2] The European Union agreed not to subject Russian goods to volume limits, with the exception of generally accepted protective measures in common use around the world—textiles are subject to limits, for example, as are steel products, designated as such under the regulations of the European Coal and Steel Community (ECSC). However, Russia's raw materials export profile is the only one that is clear to enter the EU market in practice.

Russia is taking the steps necessary to eliminate obstacles to the development of our economic ties with the European Union, in particular, to counteract the EU's antidumping measures. Since it considers Russia—despite the reality—to be a "nonmarket economy," the European Commission applies these procedures to Russia in a discriminatory fashion. Antidumping duties on Russian imports increase consumer prices for Russian goods so much that they become noncompetitive. This is true for seamless pipe, potassium chloride, and ferroalloys, for instance. In addition to this, sanctions against individual companies and enterprises in some cases extend to an entire sector of the national economy, a situation that costs Russia an estimated $300 million each year.[3]

On April 27, 1998, the EU Council resolved to take Russia and China off its list of nonmarket economies, and accordingly, to reevaluate the European Union's antidumping rules. Although this resolution was limited in scope and stipulated many conditions, it represented the first positive step on this issue. New antidumping rules went into effect July 1, 1998. However, as subsequent action by the European Commission demonstrated, continued efforts are necessary for the commission to fully acknowledge our market economy. Russian industrial exports continue to suffer from restrictions based on trade technicalities and primarily specifications (in aviation technology, automobiles, machine tools, and chemicals). Environmental restrictions and requirements are also becoming more severe. It is possible that these negative tendencies will gain strength as the European Union expands.

These conditions make it more important to implement the Medium-Term Strategy for Development of Relations between the Russian

Federation and the European Union (2000–10), released by President Putin in June 2000. A priority area for development outlined in this document is the cultivation of mutual trade and investment. The strategy clearly designates Russia's national interests for its market economy and formally states Russia's intention to expand cooperation with the EU.[4] This presents Russian diplomacy with some serious challenges:

—to achieve full recognition of our market economy

—to make EU markets more accessible to Russian goods and services

—to remove discriminatory aspects of EU trade policy

—to shape a positive view within the EU toward Russia's entry into the WTO

To meet these objectives requires serious domestic and international efforts. The joint development of a concept for a unified economic space already under way by Russia and the European Union is also of critical significance.

Another significant development is Russia's entry into the powerful intergovernmental Asia-Pacific Economic Cooperation forum. From an economic viewpoint, Russia can use APEC resources to seek resolution of economic development issues by

—becoming involved in integration processes

—diversifying economic ties

—cultivating exports to other APEC countries

—enriching our export profile

—tapping into investment flows

—representing our national interests in the development of international trade law

By joining APEC, Russia sends the international community a clear signal of its orientation toward creating an open economy. History shows that trade liberalization and investment do much to stimulate export sectors and help bolster an economy. Russia may feel the effects of liberalization most keenly in those sectors of the economy where we have heavy exports, such as energy, lumber and wood processing, fishing and other seafood, and the chemical products industry. Investment liberalization within APEC will help attract the foreign capital that is so vital for our economic development. Reduced expenses resulting from liberalization, and the simplification, standardization, and increased transparency of import-export procedures will represent direct benefits for consumers and for Russian producers alike, and will act as an added stimulus to develop more competitive domestic production.

Discussing liberalization now, at this current difficult stage of Russian economic development, seems more like wishful thinking than a concrete plan of action. Obviously, for many industry sectors and areas of the Russian economy, protective measures for national production represent a more important issue than liberalization, which seems less proactive. Yet there is no doubt that the trend toward liberalization is a permanent fixture in international economic relations. To reject outright the idea of gradual, stepwise, and measured liberalization would be as grave a mistake as jumping headlong into its rushing current. For Russia, embracing APEC processes is like buying a suit with room to grow. Although the suit may seem a little too big for Russia now, with our troubled economy, tomorrow, when our economy gains some heft, it will fit just fine.

Russia's position on membership in APEC was laid out on the eve of the Kuala Lumpur summit, in an individual plan of action for trade and investment liberalization prepared by the joint efforts of nearly forty federal ministries and agencies and endorsed by the Russian government. This document described the primary guidelines for fine-tuning and nationally coordinating adjustments to our foreign economic activities and for bringing these activities into line with standard global practice, all with consideration of our economy's current capabilities and Russia's eventual membership in the WTO.

Other important areas where Russian diplomatic efforts intersect with foreign economic issues are in the active support of Russian business abroad and in working to ensure a favorable foreign policy climate for increased foreign investment in the Russian economy.

The main prerequisite for improving our country's investment climate is, above all, the implementation of a collection of domestic measures to increase the transparency and predictability of our economic policies, to provide a firm legal foundation, and to further consolidate legislation covering foreign investment. In particular, we need to adopt a new tax code that not only meets our budgetary needs, but also stimulates investment. The implementation of other important mechanisms, like legislation on agreements governing production allotments and protecting the rights of foreign investors, is also necessary. In addition, we will be undertaking serious measures to fight crime and corruption. The implementation of all these measures must be accompanied by foreign policy efforts to increase stability with regard to Russia's leading economic partners, to build trust and increase predictability in our relations with them, and to improve the world's image of the Russian state.

Because the world economy is extremely complex and is evolving quickly, Russia's external economic strategy will undergo constant analysis and refinement. Adjustments must be based on realistic assessments of the Russian economy's capabilities and on the outlook for its projected development in the next few years. In particular, we must develop long-range measures to guard against Russia being left on the periphery of the world economy and becoming an appendage for the supply of raw materials to developed countries.

An effective foreign policy strategy depends on reshaping the social structure of Russia to correspond to the new global situation. This might entail, for instance, the formation of highly competitive economic sectors capable of effective participation in the world market and having protected sources of raw materials. As events in the Pacific Rim demonstrate, excessive dependency on global markets during crisis periods is no less dangerous than closed autarky. As it shapes viable institutions to protect itself from the variable world financial market, Russia can also increase intra-economic stability by cultivating an economic presence in countries and regions of the world where there is already a historical connection and precedent.

Given the exceptionally serious problems and challenges facing Russia's economy in the twenty-first century, we can assume that developing and refining foreign policy instruments designed to improve the economy will be one of the thorniest problems for Russian diplomacy in the coming years.

The Russian Regions and Foreign Policy

Direct regional ties make up an ever-growing component of Russia's bilateral relations with foreign states. These ties and contacts have increased in number, they cover a wider geography, and their content has become much fuller. Russian regions increasingly display the general European and global tendency for accelerated development of multilateral ties at various levels: with local authorities, provincial bodies, local communities, and various elements of civil society.

This process began in the early 1990s with great difficulty, due to the sudden and utterly unprepared entry of Russian "subjects of the Federation" into direct contact with foreign partners, often with no clear political or legal framework whatsoever to guide the process. Thus, in the early stages, the primary task of Russian diplomacy was to help the regions—which had long been totally insulated from the outside world—make mutually beneficial international contacts that did not damage the Russian Federation's unity or integrity. In other words, it was imperative to find the optimal formula for joining Russia's national interests and the interests of regions together under one foreign policy umbrella.

Today, everyone understands that expanding the foreign ties of the "subjects of the Federation" is healthy and natural. Transforming our society and carrying out reforms logically results in a transfer of the center of balance in some issues from the national to the regional or local levels. Still, this process demands very complex and painstaking efforts to identify the fine balancing line between federal and regional authority in foreign ties, especially with respect to domestic legislation and international legal standards. We must strike a balance between the interests of the Federation as a whole and those of its parts, help the "subjects of the Federation" forge more effective foreign ties, and bring regional interests into the mechanism for implementing Russian foreign policy.

The balance of authority between the federal center and "subjects of the Federation" in this area is not a theoretical issue. The issue is of great practical significance, since it must be adequately resolved for economic cooperation between regions or "subjects of the Federation" and the outside world to be effective. Skillful and well-informed management of these ties and contacts strengthens the whole of the Russian state, while parochial attitudes and pretensions of autonomy do much damage to the interests and authority of the regions themselves, as well as to the Federation as a whole.

Russia's Constitution designates foreign policy and international relations to be the exclusive purview of the Federation (Article 71). At the same time, the coordination of international and foreign economic contacts, and the implementation of international treaties, is the joint responsibility of the Federation and its entities (Article 72). This does not mean that "subjects of the Federation" are barred from developing or participating in Russia's international cooperative projects and programs. Republic and *oblast* leaders travel abroad as head of Russian delegations and sign important documents on behalf of the Russian government. Not infrequently, they also accompany the president of Russia on official visits abroad.

Issues of interaction between the Federation's center and its entities in foreign economic relations have been addressed in the Law of the Russian Federation on State Regulation of Foreign Trade Activity, in the Law on International Treaties, and in several other normative acts. However, the legislative base is still in development. Existing holes in the national legislation are partially filled by standards set at the regional level, but unfortunately not always with complete success. Naturally, federal bodies cannot permit these standards to remain in force when they contradict the Constitution or Russian federal law.

A significant milestone in improving Russian legislation in this area was the signing of the Federal Law on Coordination of International and Foreign Economic Affairs of Subjects of the Russian Federation by the president on January 4, 1999.[5] This timely action did much to stimulate international cooperation at the regional level and to increase its effectiveness in meeting Russia's national interests.

In light of the fact that approximately half of the Federation's entities share land or marine borders with neighboring states, cross-border cooperation has great significance for Russia. The dynamic development of this kind of cooperation is largely due to the nature of international affairs at this particular moment in their evolution. Direct contacts between border regions everywhere on the European continent received a simultaneous boost, when the "Europe of Regions" became a reality. Particularly interesting is the experience of Western Europe in creating integrated regional bodies—so-called Euroregions—which have joint bodies for resolving common issues. In the development of large multi-lateral projects, such regions can do much to create an environment favorable to foreign investment. The significance of this kind of cooperation between states does much more than simply meet local interests. Cross-border and regional cooperation directly answers the urgent day-to-day needs of citizens, and its fruits have a substantial impact on the overall political climate between states.

Cooperation of this kind was very significant for Russia, since it primarily involved regions that had previously been very isolated from any kind of international contact. Increased border cooperation resulted in practical solutions for many issues, such as organizing cross-border trade, simplifying border crossings, establishing new points for people and goods to cross borders, and infrastructure development, among others. Because of these efforts, many border regions in Russia have changed substantially: the Russian north and northwest regions, Kaliningrad, the Russian Far East, and Primorye.

In recent years, significant cooperative efforts have been made between the Karelia and Murmansk regions and their cross-border neighboring localities in Finland and Norway. This cooperation has been both at the bilateral level and within the framework of the subregional Barents Euro-Arctic Council. Cooperative efforts are starting to increase in the Kaliningrad, Leningrad, and other northwest regions within the analogous Baltic organization, the Council of the Baltic Sea States.

With Russian diplomatic assistance, the Black Sea Economic Cooperation (BSEC) has started to become more active. The BSEC maintains multilateral subregional contacts between a wide circle of Black Sea states and Russia's southern regions.

New opportunities have resulted from the Agreement on Partnership and Cooperation between Russia and the European Union. One of the articles of this agreement (article 73) stipulates directly that the two sides will facilitate regional development and contacts between their corresponding regions.[6]

The participation of Russian regions in multilateral regional and subregional organizations opens up additional opportunities to improve legislative mechanisms for regulating cross-border cooperation. Russia's joining the 1980 European Outline Convention on Transfrontier Cooperation between Territorial Communities or Authorities could provide substantial progress.[7] Other promising opportunities should result from the signing of interstate umbrella agreements that set the framework and scope for cooperation between regions and local authorities.

When principles of federalism are put into practice there are two opposing dangers. On one side, there is the danger of rigid centralization, and on the other side, the risk of complete disintegration and devolution of all real authority to regional entities. To avoid both extremes, it is necessary to maintain the openness and flexibility of federal structures and to guarantee a unified territorial, juridical, and economic space for the federation as a whole. A required condition for this is adherence to a national legislative base and observance of Russian law, standards, and regulations.

Interregional, cross-border ties between entities of the Russian Federation and CIS member-states deserve constant attention. When integration within the CIS begins to occur at different rates for different states, it will become critical for Russia to cultivate bilateral cooperation with CIS member-states. By extending their interregional contacts, "subjects of the Federation" are helping to achieve a strategic goal: they are reinforcing the fabric of relationships between Russia and other Commonwealth states. Obviously, trade and economics will continue to dominate interregional ties. There is much promise, too, in having the regions create their own economic cooperation associations. This would broaden the scope of cooperation and increase possibilities, and it would also significantly reduce the disturbing problem of unjustified competition for Russian regions in foreign markets, a situation that some foreign trading partners use to unfair advantage. At present, Federation associations are taking only their first, tentative steps in this field.

While the economy should get its due, we must not forget about other such aspects of interregional ties as cultural exchange and humanitarian contacts. Russia and other Commonwealth states share a close spiritual and cultural history that represents valuable strategic capital. This closeness has not yet been lost, but joint efforts are needed to preserve it. In some cases, these issues are more easily and effectively addressed at the regional level than at the national level. "Subjects of the Federation" could play a greater role in defending the interests of Russian citizens living abroad or in the "near abroad."[8]

In addition to legal activities within their own borders, "subjects of the Federation" could enter into bilateral international agreements on regional cooperation that the central government in Russia has not yet entered into with CIS member-states. Experience with these types of agreements between specific regions with China, Finland, and other countries, has shown them to be quite effective for regulating regional contacts. Within intergovernmental commissions, the creation of special groups focusing solely on interregional cooperation has shown merit.

A coordinated effort within the CIS will, however, be needed to lay the basis for effective coordination of legislation regulating interregional cross-border contacts and cooperation. The CIS Interparliamentary Assembly could play a substantial role in this by expanding programs to develop model laws based on its own example. This would be useful, for example, in the regulation of cross-border contacts.

Diplomacy and Culture

The present stage in the evolution of international relations is characterized by a substantial expansion of the range of issues that need to be addressed in multilateral and bilateral cooperation between states. In a globalized world, the breadth of these cooperative efforts essentially encompasses every area of human endeavor. The intellectual sphere is well represented by initiatives in science, education, culture, communication, and so on. In the contemporary world, a state's international authority and standing, as well as familiar characteristics like its economic and military power, are all increasingly determined by the quality of the its intellectual resources and by how attractive its development models for science, education, and culture are to other countries. Russian culture has enormous global significance and our achievements in science and education are well known. Yet there are those around the world who try to propagate extremely biased and negative images of Russia, clearly for the purpose of hindering partnerships with us. This issue is of great concern in our foreign policy.

Russian diplomacy is replete with the intellectual experiences of those in its service, both in other cultures abroad and at home in Russia. Throughout our history, the connection between diplomacy and culture has always been intimate and organic. There is a long tradition of Russia's leading writers and intellectuals serving in the ranks of the diplomatic service. Prince Antioch Kantemir (1708–44), Russian ambassador to England and to France, was one of Russia's first vernacular writers and poets. Other notable figures from Russian literature with a connection to the diplomatic service include Aleksandr Griboedov (1795–1829), Denis Fonvizin (1745–92), Konstantin Batyushkov (1787–1855), and Feodor Tyutchev (1803–73).[9] After graduating from the Lyceum in Tsarskoe Selo, Russia's greatest poet, Aleksandr S. Pushkin (1799–1837), was given a post in the Ministry of Foreign Affairs in Petersburg.

Today, the interconnection between Russian diplomacy and culture is growing considerably. Democratic reforms have emancipated Russian culture and given it an environment in which it is free to develop and engage naturally with the cultural process around the globe. At the same time, culture, education, and science have largely been commercialized, which threatens to lower their quality. Many cultural and intellectual programs have been stripped of state support that they cannot exist without. The long-term consequences of low-grade pop culture flooding into Russia from the West and the "brain drain" of talent from Russia to the West are turning into serious problems.

These circumstances challenge Russian diplomacy to support our culture, science, and education by creating more favorable conditions for their inclusion in international relations. Understandably, solving these problems requires deep understanding of the current situation within these fields, as well as close contact with leaders and prominent figures in these areas. This realization led to the creation in 1999 of the Leadership Council for Russian Science, Education, and Culture under the auspices of the Ministry of Foreign Affairs. With the direct participation of this council, a report was produced on the primary areas of effort by the ministry in developing cultural ties between Russia and foreign countries.

Never before in Russian diplomacy has there been a conceptual document that so fully and completely details the importance of culture in securing Russia's international authority and positive image in the world. Long familiar in other nations, the concept of a "cultural foreign policy" is finally taking hold here and becoming part of Russia's diplomatic practice.

Based on past experience and contemporary realities, Russia's cultural foreign policy combines traditional approaches with new areas of activity. Traditionally, Russia has a long history of bilateral cultural cooperation with foreign countries, and most of these efforts have produced agreements outlining frameworks for exchange. The implementation of these exchanges reflects the enormous domestic changes that have occurred in Russian cultural policy. Most of these exchanges are decentralized and carried out by the private sector, without any state framework. However, the absence of government involvement does not in any way preclude Russian diplomacy from supporting the development of these kinds of programs. In particular, Russian embassies around the world are frequently called on to intervene when our cultural groups run into difficulty or have problems with foreign partners who are less than conscientious.

Interaction with other CIS countries figures prominently in Russia's cultural foreign policy, and it is here that the important political function of this kind of cultural cooperation is most evident. Cultural exchange programs with the other members of the CIS preserve and strengthen the historic and spiritual connection with those states whose continuing good relations with Russia remain a priority. Cultural exchange is destined to play a big role in bringing people of the CIS closer together in a new, democratic environment. Shared efforts to promote culture can help lay the foundation for effective cooperation in other areas.

In practice this is sometimes quite difficult to attain. Cultural efforts—for instance, in promoting the study and use of the Russian language, or creating educational communities and networks of specialized technical schools—desperately need government support and protection. Russia supports and assists in meeting the cultural and educational needs of our foreign nationals living in the near abroad. This requires centralized efforts as part of a larger unified state strategy for supporting Russian nationals who work and reside abroad.

Experience over recent years has demonstrated that in any successful cultural foreign policy the greatest effect is produced by large, complex cultural activities involving many countries and a wide circle of diverse foreign cultural groups. Such events are frequently associated with an anniversary commemorating a particular event or central figure in

Russian culture. The series of events held in Russia and abroad to commemorate the 200th anniversary of the birth of Aleksandr Pushkin is one such example that had considerable impact. These commemorative events were carried out with the direct involvement of the Ministry of Foreign Affairs and many Russian embassies. The celebration was observed all around the world and was truly exceptional in its scope and diversity. In addition to numerous conferences, exhibits, and international competitions dedicated to this great Russian poet, many cities around the world also erected permanent monuments to Pushkin, and the UNESCO Executive Committee—representing over fifty states—unanimously adopted a special resolution to recognize this anniversary. Thus, foreign celebrations of Pushkin's life not only demonstrated worldwide respect for Russian literature, but also significantly contributed to improving Russia's image in the world.

Globalization makes it more important for Russia to participate in multilateral dialogue and cooperation in the fields of education, science, and culture. Russia's traditional partner in these areas is one of the most respected and well-liked arms of the United Nations: UNESCO. Russia has a long history of fruitful cooperation with UNESCO. In today's complex international situation, UNESCO has remained true to its original noble mission—to serve the interests of the "intellectual and moral solidarity of mankind." The ideas and conceptual output mobilized by UNESCO toward nurturing the spirit of peace around the world and preserving the cultural diversity of human civilization have received broad international recognition and have been manifested in multilateral projects and programs too numerous to count. A measure of this recognition is the UN General Assembly's adoption of UNESCO's Declaration and Plan of Action for World Culture.

UNESCO's activities and the values that lie at the organization's core serve to refute the widely voiced fatalistic Western view that the "clash of civilizations" is inevitable. If such a conflict were to occur, it would be the result of an exceptional attempt by one nation to force its ideology and cultural values upon others. Luckily, the overwhelming majority of the world community is committed to realizing—with the tool of international relations—the principle of human civilization's unity in diversity.

Russia actively supports UNESCO because we believe that in its modus operandi—cultural and intellectual exchange and cooperation—we will find solutions to serious world problems, including mankind's inability to rein in the negative side effects of scientific and technological progress, the widening gap between developed and less-developed countries, and the erosion of moral values. Russia actively participates in UNESCO's international programs in such areas as improving and humanizing education, educating youth for peace, democracy and human rights, the education of refugees and marginalized youth, and the ethics of scientific and technological progress, especially in the area of genetic engineering, computer science, and communications technology.

The borders between universal and national values in science, culture, and education today are becoming harder and harder to discern. This is why we value so highly UNESCO's support of scientific research and higher education in Russia, especially the support extended to the Hermitage Museum, the Russian National Library, the Bolshoi Theater, as well as other projects designed to preserve World Heritage Sites in Russia. Although we stand in solidarity with all these efforts on our behalf, they represent an investment in the preservation of the cultural property and intellectual potential of all mankind.

Diplomacy as Science

Modern diplomacy, which must cope with the demands of the present stage in the evolution of international relations, as well as with a whole new range of issues that require international cooperation in order to be solved, needs to completely overhaul its professional toolbox. The old methods are no longer adequate. This encompasses not only the forms and methods of diplomatic activity, but also the manner in which we educate and train our diplomats today.

There is insufficient space here to fully explore all aspects of this problem, which really deserves a separate, comprehensive examination. At this point, I will just touch on the basic directions in which diplomatic activity is evolving. These evolutionary changes stem from the demands of the transitional period that international relations are now experiencing.

Diplomatic efforts in economics, information science, and culture are all critical, as mentioned earlier. An overarching concern, though, is that the intellectual component of diplomacy must be increased in a broad way. Although diplomacy is challenged by the need to analyze and process more and more information from a wider array of sources, it is increasingly necessary to take into account the interests of other states and of the world community. In other words, creating a foreign policy course based solely on one nation's "selfish" interests (and supported by the traditional instruments of economic or military might) will lead directly to a clash with the realities of an increasingly globalized and interdependent world. This means that the modern diplomat must learn the art of negotiation and how to harmonize his or her own state's interests with the broad interests of the whole global community.

Specifically, a greater role needs to be created for intellectual examination, research, and analysis; in other words, a new balance must be sought between diplomacy as a professional "art" and diplomacy as a "science." In recent years, this type of interaction has gradually become an integral component in the way major foreign policy decisions are made. Experience shows that no diplomatic agency can conduct policy without a solid informational and analytical background. Many foreign affairs offices around the world have research institutes or think tanks attached to them, and Russia is no exception. Within the Ministry of Foreign Affairs, we created the Analytical Council, which periodically meets to make recommendations to the leadership regarding specific trends or elements of diplomatic practice. The council is made up of prominent academics and directors from many different university and academic centers.

The institutions which will permit diplomacy and science to interact will improve in the future, dictated by our need to find responses to the challenges of modern international life that require more in-depth and expert analysis.

CONCLUSION

The foreign policy of Russia, like the entire course of international relations itself, is an ongoing, dynamic, and creative process. After turning the final page of this book, it is important to realize that this is not in any way the final word on the subject; the process described therein will never be finished.

The mechanism by which the foreign policy of any state is developed can be conceived of in mathematical terms, as a formula containing closely related "constants" and "variables." A state's basic interests, goals, and aspirations represent the constants. The variables are the whole array of changeable internal and external factors, constantly in flux, against which the state needs to coordinate its practical efforts in the international arena. At all times, the constants and the variables must be in balance. If the formula is too weighted on the side of the constants, the result is a foreign policy based on doctrine, possessing little flexibility. If it is biased toward the variables, the opposite emerges: an unprincipled foreign policy that reacts to every little shift in international affairs.

In 1991, entering the international arena with a new geopolitical cast, Russia had to answer several fundamental questions, both for itself and for the world. What were its core national interests? How did it conceive of its place and role in global affairs? We soon learned that finding the answers to these questions would be a long and difficult process.

Today, since the constants in Russia's foreign policy are largely known, we are focusing on fine-tuning the institutions for implementing the "real-life" interests of Russian foreign policy. In so doing, these institutions strive to meet the demands of today's complex and constantly evolving system of international relations.

We live in a time when the technology and the tools of foreign policy and diplomacy are constantly being reinvented. A century ago, international relations was largely limited to the geographical confines of Europe, and in reality consisted of the interrelationships of five or six leading powers. Foreign policy was developed and carried out by an elite group of individuals and, as a rule, hidden from any public scrutiny. Directors of the diplomatic agencies never had more than a handful of international issues in their sights at any one time.

The twentieth century changed this situation enormously, and international relations became more complex than ever before. Today, the world community is composed of approximately 200 independent states, as well as dozens of international organizations engaged in the widest variety of cooperative efforts at regional and global levels. World affairs are increasingly influenced not only by large financial and industrial corporations, but by the media as well. Another influential force is the involvement in international relations of a vast number of new, nongovernmental participants—essentially an international civil society.

Russian foreign policy and diplomacy of the twenty-first century must be seen and understood in the context of this new, wildly developing structure of international relations. Globalization makes powerful incursions into all facets of modern society, and scholars who study this process agree that it is erasing the boundaries between external (foreign) and internal (domestic) policy. One sign of this is the interconnection— tighter now than at any time previously—between foreign policy goals and domestic development priorities. This idea lies at the heart of Russia's Foreign Policy Concept. Everything we do today in the field of foreign policy has one overarching purpose: to create the most favorable conditions possible for consistent development of the Russian economy and our society. Foreign policy is shifting its position to face the realities of life head on. A growing proportion of foreign policy goals are, therefore, oriented toward people: protection of the interests of Russian citizens and compatriots abroad; active support for Russian businesses trying to enter foreign markets; and development of international contacts in culture, science, and other areas.

Logically, this means that, in a certain sense, all of society has begun to participate in foreign policy, not just a diplomatic elite. This is why an important aspect of any successful foreign policy will continue to be the support it receives from Russian public opinion. This requires the emergence of a broad consensus among political forces as to the main goals of Russian foreign policy, and a greater flow of useful information to society at large. In turn, a high level of feedback from a public informed and enlightened on issues of foreign policy will be essential to Russian diplomacy in the future. The Russian academic community, therefore, will need to play an important role in creating this level of public input. Foreign policy in a globalized world will certainly require a higher level of scholarly analysis. We will need better models for predicting long-range trends in international relations and for incorporating them into policy practice.

In years past, one would refer to the "art of diplomacy," focusing on the role of the individual practitioner. Without diminishing this phrase, we may find that a more appropriate characterization for the coming century will be "diplomatic science," emphasizing the importance of institutions and processes.

A stronger, organic relationship between diplomacy and science is an imperative of our time. The author sincerely hopes that the goal of this book—to examine the lessons that can be learned from new Russia's first decade of foreign policy experience—will continue to provide material for further in-depth research. Such research will help to further the conversation on Russia's foreign policy goals and its place and role in the international system of the future.

Foreign Policy Concept
of the Russian Federation

I. General Provisions

The Foreign Policy Concept of the Russian Federation is a system of views of the substance of and the guideline for the foreign policy activities of Russia.

The legal framework of this Concept is provided by the Constitution of the Russian Federation, federal laws, other regulatory legal acts of the Russian Federation that govern the activities of the federal bodies of government in the domain of foreign policy, the universally recognized principles and norms of international law, and the international treaties of the Russian Federation, as well as by the National Security Concept of the Russian Federation, as approved by Decree 24 of the President of the Russian Federation, of January 10, 2000.

The international situation by the beginning of the twenty-first century has required a rethinking of the overall situation around the Russian Federation, the priorities of Russian foreign policy, and the resources available to support it. Along with the strengthening of the international positions of the Russian Federation, some negative tendencies have manifested themselves. Some of the expectations for the emergence of new, equitable, and mutually beneficial relations of partnership between Russia and the surrounding world, as set forth in the Basic Provisions of the Foreign Policy Concept of the Russian Federation, approved by Directive 248-rp of the President of the Russian Federation on April 23, 1993, and in other documents, have not materialized.

The uppermost priority of the foreign policy course of Russia is protection of the interests of the individual, society, and the state. Within the framework of this process, the main efforts should be directed toward attaining the following principal objectives:

—ensuring reliable security of the country and preserving and strengthening its sovereignty and territorial integrity and its strong and respected position in the world community, as would best of all meet the interests of the Russian Federation as a great power and influential center in the modern world and is central to the growth of its political, economic, intellectual and spiritual potential;

—influencing world processes with the aim of shaping a stable, just, and democratic world order, one based on the universally recognized norms of international law—including, first of all, the goals and principles of the UN Charter—and also on equitable relations of partnership among states;

—creating favorable external conditions for the progressive development of Russia, for its economic growth, for raising living standards, for the successful implementation of democratic change, for strengthening the foundations of the constitutional system, and for respect for human rights and freedoms;

—forming a belt of good-neighborliness along the perimeter of Russia's borders and helping to extinguish the existing seats of tension and conflicts and prevent the emergence of potential ones in regions adjacent to the Russian Federation;

—searching for accord and common interests with foreign countries and interstate associations in the process of tackling the tasks stemming from Russia's national priorities, and building, on this basis, a system of relations of partnership and alliance that would improve the conditions and parameters of international collaboration;

—ensuring comprehensive protection of the rights and interests of Russian citizens and compatriots abroad;

—promoting a positive perception of the Russian Federation in the world and the popularization of the Russian language and cultures of the peoples of Russia in foreign states.

II. The Contemporary World and the Foreign Policy of the Russian Federation

The contemporary world is going through fundamental and dynamic change that profoundly affects the interests of the Russian Federation and its citizens. Russia is an active participant in this process. As a permanent member of the UN Security Council, possessing substantial potential and resources in every sphere of life, and maintaining intensive relations with the leading states of the world, Russia exerts substantial influence on the formation of a new world order.

The transformation of international relations, the end of confrontation and continuous progress in overcoming the consequences of the cold war, and the advance of Russian reform have substantially broadened possibilities for cooperation in the world arena. The threat of a global nuclear conflict has been minimized. While military force is still important in relations between states, an ever greater role is being played by economic, political, scientific, technological, environmental, and information factors. Coming to the fore as the main components of the national might of the Russian Federation are its intellectual, information, and communications capabilities, the well-being and educational standards of its people, the degree to which its scientific and production resources dovetail, the concentration of financial capital, and the diversification of economic ties. The overwhelming majority of nations are by now firmly committed to the methods of the market economy and to democratic values. Major breakthroughs in a number of key areas of scientific and technological progress, resulting in the formation of a single worldwide information environment, and the deepening and diversification of international economic ties are lending a global dimension to the interdependence of states. Prerequisites are being created for building up a more stable and crisis-proof world architecture.

At the same time, new challenges and threats to the national interests of Russia are emerging in the international sphere. A trend is growing toward the establishment of a unipolar world structure that would be dominated by the United States economically and through force. There is a focus on restricted-membership Western institutions and forums in addressing fundamental issues of international security, with a weakening role of the UN Security Council.

The strategy of unilateral action can destabilize the international situation, provoke tensions and an arms race, and exacerbate the contradictions between states and national and religious strife. The use of force-based methods in circumvention of the existing international legal mechanisms is incapable of removing the deep-seated socioeconomic, ethnic, and other contradictions that underlie conflicts, and only undermines the foundations of the rule of law.

Russia will seek to achieve a multipolar system of international relations that would genuinely reflect the diversity of the contemporary world, with its varied interests. Such a world order can be guaranteed to be effective and durable if interests are taken into account on a reciprocal basis. The world order of the twenty-first century should be based on mechanisms for the collective resolution of key problems, on the primacy of law, and on a broad democratization of international relations. Other trends that are immediately related to Russia's interests include

—globalization of the world economy. Along with opening up additional possibilities for socioeconomic progress and for broadening human contacts, this trend gives rise to new dangers, especially for economically weakened states, and the probability of large-scale financial and economic crises is growing. The risk of the economic system and information environment of the Russian Federation becoming dependent on external influences is increasing;

—strengthening of the role of international institutions and mechanisms in the world economy and politics (G-8, the IMF, the World Bank and others), caused by the objectively growing interdependence of nations and by the need to make the international system more manageable. It is in Russia's interest to have a full and equitable role in drafting the fundamental principles that would govern the functioning of the world financial and economic system in the present conditions;

—development of regional and subregional integration in Europe, the Asia-Pacific region, Africa, and Latin America. Associations based on integration are acquiring an ever-greater importance in the world economy and are becoming a significant factor of regional and subregional security and peacemaking;

—military-political rivalry among regional powers and the rise of separatism and ethnic, national, and religious extremism. Integration processes, in particular in the Euro-Atlantic region, often assume a selective and restrictive character. Attempts to belittle the role of the sovereign state as a fundamental element of international relations create the threat of arbitrary interference in internal affairs. The problem of the proliferation of weapons of mass destruction and means of their delivery is acquiring serious dimensions. Ongoing or potential regional and local armed conflicts pose a threat to international peace and security. The growth of international terrorism, transnational organized crime, and illegal drug and arms trafficking are beginning to exert substantial influence on global and regional stability.

The threats related to the above trends are compounded by the fact that the resources available to support the foreign policy of the Russian Federation are limited, which makes it more difficult to successfully uphold its foreign economic interests and narrows the scope of its information and cultural influence abroad.

At the same time the Russian Federation has real potential to ensure an appropriate place for itself in the world. Further strengthening of Russia's statehood, consolidation of civil society, and speedy transition to sustained economic growth have a critical role to play in this respect.

Over the past few decades Russia has been able to tap additional opportunities for international cooperation, opportunities that are opening up as a result of fundamental change in the country, has made good progress on the road to integration in the system of world economic relations, and has joined a number of influential international organizations and institutions. Through strenuous efforts, Russia's positions in the world have been strengthened in several areas of major importance.

The Russian Federation is pursuing an independent and constructive foreign policy, one based on consistency, predictability, and mutually advantageous pragmatism. This policy is transparent to the maximum possible degree, takes into consideration the legitimate interests of other states, and is aimed at seeking joint decisions.

Russia is a reliable partner in international relations. Its constructive role in resolving acute international problems has been universally acknowledged.

A distinctive feature of Russia's foreign policy is its balanced nature. This is predicated on its geopolitical position as a major Eurasian power, which requires an optimal mix of efforts in every direction. Such an approach predetermines Russia's responsibility for maintaining security in the world at both the global and regional levels and calls for the development of foreign policy activities on a bilateral and a multilateral basis in a mutually complementary manner.

III. Priorities of the Russian Federation in Addressing Global Problems

A successful foreign policy for the Russian Federation should be based on maintaining a reasonable balance between its objectives and the possibilities of attaining them. Any focus of political, diplomatic, military, economic, financial, and other means on accomplishing foreign policy missions should be commensurate with their real significance for Russia's national interests, while the scope of participation in international affairs should be relative to the actual contribution to strengthening the country's positions. The diversity and complexity of international problems and the existence of crisis situations presuppose that the priority of each of these in the foreign policy agenda of the Russian Federation should be determined in a timely manner. It is necessary to enhance the effectiveness of political, legal, foreign economic, and other instruments in protecting Russia's state sovereignty and its national economy at a time of globalization.

1. Building a New World Architecture

Russia has an interest in a stable system of international relations, a system based on the principles of equality, mutual respect, and mutually beneficial cooperation. Such a system is called upon to ensure reliable security for each member of the world community in the political, military, economic, humanitarian and other areas.

The United Nations should remain the principal center for managing international relations in the twenty-first century. The Russian Federation will resolutely oppose any attempts to belittle the role of the United Nations and its Security Council in world affairs.

Strengthening the consolidatory role of the United Nations in the world calls for

—strict compliance with the fundamental principles of the UN Charter, including the preservation of the status of the permanent members of the UN Security Council;

—rational reform of the United Nations in order to develop its mechanism for prompt response to world developments, including the enhancement of its crisis and conflict prevention and settlement capabilities;

—further enhancement of the efficiency of the UN Security Council, which bears primary responsibility for the maintenance of international peace and security, and the imparting of a more representative character to this body by bringing in new permanent members, first and foremost, well-respected developing states. Any reform of the United Nations must proceed from the assumption that the right of veto of the permanent members of the UN Security Council is inviolable.

Russia attaches great importance to its participation in the Group of Eight leading industrialized nations. Appreciating the mechanism of consultation and harmonization of positions on the most important problems of the day as one of the substantive instruments in upholding and advancing its foreign policy interests, the Russian Federation intends to build up collaboration with partners in this forum.

2. Strengthening International Security

Russia stands for further decreasing the role played by force as a factor in international relations, with a simultaneous enhancement of strategic and regional stability. Toward this end, the Russian Federation

—will strictly respect the obligations it has assumed under the effective treaties and agreements on the limitation and reduction of armaments, and will participate in drafting and concluding new accords that would be consistent both with its national interests and with the security interests of other states;

—is prepared to further reduce its nuclear potential on the basis of bilateral agreements with the United States, and in a multilateral format, with the participation of other nuclear powers, on the condition that strategic stability in the nuclear sphere should not be upset. Russia will seek the preservation of and compliance with the 1972 Treaty on the Limitation of Anti-Ballistic Missile Systems as the cornerstone of strategic stability. The implementation by the United States of plans to create a missile defense system to defend its territory will inevitably compel the Russian Federation to take adequate measures in order to maintain its national security at an appropriate level;

—reaffirms its invariable course of participation, jointly with other states, in preventing the proliferation of nuclear weapons and other weapons of mass destruction and the means of their delivery, as well as relevant materials and technologies. The Russian Federation is an ardent supporter of reinforcing and developing the relevant international regimes, including the creation of a global system to monitor the non-proliferation of missiles and missile technology. The Russian Federation intends to firmly honor its commitments under the Comprehensive Nuclear Test Ban Treaty and urges all the world's nations to join it;

—attaches special attention to ensuring information security as an aspect of consolidating strategic stability;

—intends to further contribute to strengthening regional stability by participating in processes of reducing and limiting conventional armed forces, as well as applying confidence-building measures in the military sphere;

—regards international peace making as an effective instrument for settling armed conflicts and calls for reinforcing its legal base in strict accordance with the principles of the UN Charter. In supporting measures to build up and modernize the United Nations' potential for anti-crisis rapid response, the Russian Federation intends to continue its active participation in peacekeeping operations conducted both under the auspices of the United Nations and, in specific cases, by regional and subregional organizations. The need for and extent of such participation will be correlated with the national interests and international commitments of the country. Russia proceeds from the premise that only the UN Security Council has the authority to sanction the use of force for the purpose of enforcing peace;

—proceeds from the premise that the use of force in violation of the UN Charter is unlawful and threatens the stabilization of the entire system of international relations. Attempts to introduce concepts such as "humanitarian intervention" and "limited sovereignty" in international practice in order to justify unilateral actions of force in circumvention of the UN Security Council are unacceptable. In its readiness for substantive dialogue on upgrading the legal aspects of the use of force in international relations at a time of globalization, the Russian Federation proceeds from the assumption that any search for concrete forms of response on the part of the international community to various acute situations, including humanitarian crises, should be conducted collectively, on the basis of strict adherence to the norms of international law and the UN Charter;

—will participate in activities under the auspices of the United Nations and other international organizations in order to clear up natural and man-made disasters and other emergency situations, as well as rendering humanitarian aid to the affected countries;

—regards the fight against international terrorism, which is capable of destabilizing the situation not only in individual states but in entire regions, as a major foreign policy mission. The Russian Federation stands for the further development of measures to intensify collaboration among states in this area. It is an immediate duty for every nation to protect its citizens against terrorist encroachments, to prevent any activity on its territory that is aimed at organizing such acts against citizens and interests of other countries, and to deny asylum to terrorists;

—will purposefully fight illegal drug trafficking and the growth of organized crime in collaboration with other states in a multilateral format, primarily within the framework of specialized international agencies, as well as at a bilateral level.

3. International Economic Relations

The main priority of the foreign policy of the Russian Federation in international economic relations is to promote the development of the national economy, which at a time of globalization is unthinkable without Russia's large-scale integration in the system of world economic ties. In order to achieve this objective, it is necessary

—to ensure favorable external conditions for the formation of a market-oriented economy in the country and for the development of a renewed external economic specialization for the Russian Federation, one that would guarantee maximum economic benefit from its participation in the international division of labor;

—to minimize risks relating to the further integration of Russia in the world economy, with due regard for the need to ensure the economic security of the country;

—to promote the formation of a fair international trade system, with the full-fledged participation of the Russian Federation in international economic institutions that would ensure the protection of the national interests by such institutions;

—to encourage the expansion of domestic export and rationalization of imports into the country, as well as Russian business abroad, uphold Russian interests in foreign markets and oppose any discrimination against domestic producers and exporters, and enforce strict compliance with Russian legislation by the Russian subjects of the foreign economic activity in conducting such operations;

—to facilitate the mobilization of foreign investment, primarily in the real sector and in priority spheres of the Russian economy;

—to ensure the preservation and optimal use of Russian property abroad;

—to bring Russian foreign debt servicing into line with the real capabilities of the country and seek the maximum possible repayment of credits granted to foreign states;

—to develop a comprehensive system of Russian legislation and an international contractual and legal framework in the economic sphere.

Russia should be prepared to make use of all the economic levers and resources available to it in order to protect its national interests.

Taking into account the growing threat of global natural and man-made disasters, the Russian Federation advocates broader international cooperation in order to ensure environmental security, including through the use of state-of-the-art technologies, for the benefit of the entire international community.

4. Human Rights and International Relations

Committed to the values of democratic society, including respect for human rights and freedoms, Russia sees its goals as follows:

—to seek respect for human rights and freedoms all over the world, on the basis of compliance with the rules of international law;

—to protect the rights and interests of Russian citizens and compatriots abroad, on the basis of international law and effective bilateral agreements. The Russian Federation will seek adequate guarantees for the rights and freedoms of compatriots in states of their permanent residence and maintain and develop all-round ties with them and with their organizations;

—to develop international cooperation in the sphere of humanitarian exchanges;

—to expand participation in international conventions and agreements in the sphere of human rights;

—to continue bringing the legislation of the Russian Federation in conformity with Russia's international obligations.

5. Information Support for Foreign Policy Activities

An important area of the foreign policy activities of the Russian Federation is objectively and accurately informing broad strata of the world public about Russia's positions on key international problems, about foreign policy initiatives and actions of the Russian Federation, and also about the achievements of Russian culture, science, and intellectual endeavor. The goal of shaping a positive perception of Russia abroad and a friendly attitude toward it is becoming a priority. Purposeful efforts to explain in detail abroad the essence of Russia's domestic policies and the processes taking place in the country should be part and parcel of this work. The swift development in the Russian Federation of its own effective means of using information to exert influence on public opinion abroad is becoming an urgent goal.

IV. Regional Priorities

A priority area in Russia's foreign policy is ensuring that multilateral and bilateral cooperation with the member countries of the Commonwealth of Independent States (CIS) conforms to the national security tasks of the country.

Emphasis will be placed on the development of good-neighborly relations and strategic partnership with all the CIS member countries. Practical relations with each of them should be structured with due regard for reciprocal openness to cooperation and readiness to properly take into account the interests of the Russian Federation, including guarantees for the rights of Russian compatriots.

Proceeding from the concept of multispeed and multilevel integration within the CIS, Russia will determine the parameters and character of its interaction with CIS member countries both within the CIS as a whole and in narrower associations, primarily in the Customs Union and the Collective Security Treaty. A priority task is to strengthen the Union of Belarus and Russia as the highest form of integration of two sovereign states at this stage.

We attach prime importance to joint efforts for settling conflicts in CIS member countries and to the development of cooperation in the military and political areas and in the sphere of security, particularly in fighting international terrorism and extremism.

Serious emphasis will be placed on the development of economic cooperation, including the creation of a free trade zone and the implementation of programs of joint rational use of natural resources. Specifically, Russia will seek the formulation of a status for the Caspian Sea that would enable the littoral nations to launch mutually advantageous cooperation in developing the region's resources on a fair basis and with due regard for the legitimate interests of each other.

The Russian Federation will make efforts to ensure the fulfillment of mutual obligations as regards preserving and augmenting the common cultural heritage in CIS member countries.

Relations with European nations are Russia's traditional foreign policy priority. The main goal of Russia's foreign policy in Europe is to build a stable and democratic system of pan-European security and cooperation. Russia has an interest in the further balanced development of the multifunctional character of the Organization for Security and Cooperation in Europe (OSCE) and will make efforts in this direction. It is important to make maximum use of the regulation-making potential which that forum has accumulated since the adoption of the 1975 Helsinki Final Act and which remains fully relevant. Russia will strongly oppose any narrowing of OSCE functions, in particular, any attempts to redirect its activities toward the post-Soviet space and the Balkans.

Russia will seek to make sure that the adapted Treaty on the Conventional Armed Forces in Europe becomes an effective instrument of ensuring European security and that confidence-building measures become comprehensive, covering in particular coalition activities and naval operations.

Proceeding from its own needs in building a civil society, Russia intends to continue its participation in the activities of the Council of Europe.

Relations with the European Union (EU) are of key importance. The ongoing processes within the EU are having a growing impact on the dynamics of the situation in Europe. These include EU enlargement, transition to a common currency, institutional reform, and the emergence of joint foreign and security policies and a common defense identity. Regarding these processes as an objective component of European development, Russia will seek due respect for its interests, including in the sphere of bilateral relations with individual EU member countries.

The Russian Federation views the EU as one of its main political and economic partners and will strive to develop intensive, sustainable, and long-term cooperation with it, cooperation that would be free from any opportunistic fluctuations.

The character of relations with the EU is determined by the framework of the Agreement on Partnership and Cooperation of June 24, 1994, establishing partnerships between the Russian Federation, on the one hand, and the European Communities and their member nations, on the other; that agreement has yet to start working at full capacity. Concrete problems, primarily the problem of adequate respect for the interests of the Russian side in the process of EU enlargement and reform, will be addressed on the basis of the Strategy for the Development of Relations between the Russian Federation and the European Union, as approved in 1999. The EU's emerging military and political dimension should become a matter of particular attention.

In realistically assessing the role of the North Atlantic Treaty Organization (NATO), Russia proceeds from the importance of cooperation with it in the interests of maintaining security and stability on the continent and is open to constructive interaction. The requisite framework for that was laid down by the Founding Act on Mutual Relations, Cooperation and Security between the Russian Federation and the North Atlantic Treaty Organization, of May 27, 1997. The intensity of cooperation with NATO will depend on the latter's compliance with the key provisions of this document, primarily those concerning nonuse of force or threat of force and nondeployment of conventional armed force groupings or nuclear weapons and means of delivery thereof in the territories of new members.

However, NATO's present-day political and military goals in many ways diverge from the security interests of the Russian Federation, and occasionally directly contradict them. First of all, this concerns the postulates of NATO's new strategic concept that allow for the conduct of force-based operations outside the zone of the Washington Treaty without UN Security Council authorization. Russia continues to view the expansion of NATO negatively.

Intensive and constructive cooperation between Russia and NATO is only possible on condition of due respect for the interests of the two sides and unconditional compliance with the mutual obligations assumed.

Interaction with West European nations, primarily with such influential ones as France, Germany, Great Britain, and Italy, is an important resource for the upholding of Russia's national interests in European and world affairs and for the stabilization and growth of the Russian economy.

In relations with Central and East European countries, the preservation of traditional human, economic, and cultural ties, the overcoming of the existing crisis phenomena, and an additional impetus to cooperation in accordance with the new circumstances and Russian interests retain their relevance.

There are good prospects for the development of the Russian Federation's relations with Lithuania, Latvia, and Estonia. Russia stands for setting these relations on the track of good-neighborliness and mutually beneficial cooperation. One indispensable condition for this is respect for Russia's interests by those states, including on the central question of respect for the rights of the Russian-speaking population.

Russia will give every assistance to the attainment of a just and durable settlement of the situation in the Balkans, based on the concerted decisions of the world community. It is of fundamental importance to preserve the territorial integrity of the Federal Republic of Yugoslavia and to oppose the partition of the state—something that is fraught with the risk of an outbreak of a pan-Balkan conflict, with unpredictable consequences.

The Russian Federation stands ready to overcome considerable latter-day difficulties in relations with the United States and to preserve the infrastructure of Russian-American cooperation that has been developed over nearly the past ten years. Despite the presence of serious, and occasionally fundamental, differences, Russian-American interaction is an essential condition for improving the international situation and achieving global strategic stability.

Above all, this concerns problems of disarmament, arms control and nonproliferation of weapons of mass destruction, as well as prevention or settlement of the most dangerous regional conflicts. It is only through active dialogue with the United States that the issues of limitation and reduction of strategic nuclear weapons can be resolved. It is in our mutual interests to maintain regular bilateral contacts at all levels and to prevent pauses in relations and setbacks in negotiating processes on key political, military, and economic matters.

Asia enjoys an ever-growing importance in the context of the foreign policy of the Russian Federation, due to the fact that Russia is literally a part of this dynamically developing region and to the need for economic uplift in Siberia and the Far East. Emphasis will be placed on the invigoration of Russia's participation in the main integration structures of the Asia-Pacific region—the Asia-Pacific Economic Cooperation forum, the regional security forum of the Association of Southeast Asian Nations (ASEAN), and the Shanghai Five (Russia, China, Kazakhstan, Kirghizia, and Tajikistan), established with Russia's initiative and active role.

The development of relations of friendship with the leading Asian nations, primarily China (PRC) and India, constitutes a major goal for Russian foreign policy in Asia. The concurrence of the fundamental approaches of Russia and the PRC to the key issues of world politics is one of the basic mainstays of regional and global stability. Russia seeks to develop mutually advantageous cooperation with China in all areas. The main task is, as before, to bring the scale of economic interaction into line with the level of political relations.

Russia intends to strengthen its traditional partnership with India, including in international affairs, and to help overcome problems persisting in South Asia and strengthen stability in the region.

Russia views the signing by India and Pakistan of the Comprehensive Nuclear Test-Ban Treaty and their accession to the Treaty on the Non-Proliferation of Nuclear Weapons as an important factor of stability in the Asia-Pacific region. It will support the creation of nuclear weapon–free zones in Asia.

The Russian Federation favors the sustainable development of relations with Japan and the attainment of true good-neighborliness, which would meet the national interests of both countries. Within the framework of the existing negotiating mechanisms, Russia will continue to seek a mutually acceptable solution regarding the formal recognition of an internationally recognized border between the two states.

Russian foreign policy is aimed at building up positive momentum in relations with the states of South-East Asia.

It is important to continue developing relations with Iran.

The overall improvement of the situation in Asia, where the geopolitical ambitions of a number of states are growing, the arms race is escalating, and seats of tensions and conflicts persist, is of fundamental importance to Russia. The situation on the Korean Peninsula is of particular concern. Efforts will be focused on assuring Russia's equitable participation in the solution of the Korean problem and on maintaining balanced relations with both Korean states.

The protracted conflict in Afghanistan poses a real threat to the security of the southern borders of the CIS and directly affects Russia's interests. Russia, in cooperation with the other states concerned, will make consistent efforts toward achieving a lasting and fair political settlement of the Afghan problem and preventing the export of terrorism and extremism from that country.

Russia will seek stabilization of the situation in the Middle East, including the Persian Gulf zone and North Africa, taking into account the impact of the regional situation on the world situation as a whole. Using its status as a cosponsor of the peace process, Russia intends to pursue a policy line for active participation in the normalization of the postcrisis situation in the region. Russia's priority in this context will be to restore and strengthen its positions, particularly economic ones, in a region of the world that is so rich and important for our interests.

Viewing the Greater Mediterranean as a hub of such regions as the Middle East, the Black Sea, the Caucasus, and the Caspian, Russia intends to steer a purposeful course toward turning it into a zone of peace, stability, and good-neighborliness, which will help advance Russia's economic interests, including the choice of routes for major energy flows.

Russia will expand interaction with African states and contribute to an early settlement of regional military conflicts in Africa. It is also necessary to promote political dialogue with the Organization of African Unity (OAU) and subregional organizations and to use their capabilities to enable Russia to join in multilateral economic projects on the continent.

Russia seeks a higher level of political dialogue and economic cooperation with the countries of Central and South America, relying on serious progress achieved in its relations with this region in the 1990s. In particular, it will seek to expand interactions with nations of Central and South America in international organizations, to encourage Russian science-intensive industrial exports to Latin American countries, and to develop military and technical cooperation.

In defining regional priorities in its foreign policy, the Russian Federation will take into account the intensity of and trends in the formation of the major world centers and the degree to which their members are ready to broaden bilateral interaction with Russia.

V. Formulation and Implementation of Foreign Policy of the Russian Federation

The President of the Russian Federation, in conformity with his constitutional powers, provides guidance for the country's foreign policy and, as head of state, represents the Russian Federation in international relations.

The Council of Federation and the State Duma of the Federal Assembly of the Russian Federation, within the framework of their constitutional powers, pursue legislative work to support the foreign policy course of the Russian Federation and fulfillment of its international obligations.

The Security Council of the Russian Federation drafts decisions of the President of the Russian Federation in the area of international security and monitors their implementation.

The Ministry of Foreign Affairs of the Russian Federation carries out work for the direct implementation of the foreign policy course approved by the President of the Russian Federation. The Foreign Ministry of Russia coordinates foreign policy activities pursued by federal executive authorities and monitors them in accordance with Decree 375 by the President of the Russian Federation, On the Coordinating Role of the Ministry of Foreign Affairs of the Russian Federation in the Conduct of Unified Foreign Policy Line of the Russian Federation, of March 12, 1996.

The constituent entities of the Russian Federation shall pursue their international ties in accordance with the Constitution of the Russian Federation, the Federal Law on Coordination of International and External Economic Ties of the Constituent Entities of the Russian Federation and other legislative acts. The Foreign Ministry of Russia and other federal executive authorities render assistance to constituent entities of the Russian Federation in their international cooperation with strict respect for the sovereignty and territorial integrity of the Russian Federation.

While preparing decisions on the conduct of the state's foreign policy course, the federal executive authorities cooperate, if necessary, with nongovernmental organizations of Russia. A more extensive involvement of nongovernmental organizations in the country's foreign policy activities is consistent with the task of ensuring maximum support by civil society for government foreign policy and is capable of contributing to its effective implementation.

Consistent implementation of foreign policy will create favorable conditions for the fulfillment of the historic choice of the peoples of the Russian Federation in favor of a state based on the rule of law, a democratic society, and a socially oriented market economy.

NOTES

Explanatory notes have been added by the editor.

To the American Reader

1. S. D. Sazonov, *Vospominaniya*, Moscow, 1991, pp. 346–47.

Chapter One

1. President Vladimir Putin, Annual Address to the Federal Assembly of the Russian Federation, the Kremlin, Moscow, April 3, 2001, p. 40.

2. The Russian-language text of the Concept can be found in *Rossiiskaya gazeta*, July 11, 2000.

3. See *Sobranie zakonodatel'stva Rossiiskoi Federatsii, 2000*, no. 2, p. 690–704.

4. The Russian Federation is a federal state composed of eighty-nine republics, territories, regions, and autonomous areas (Article 65 of the Constitution); foreign policy is defined as being in the sole jurisdiction of the federal government (Article 71).

5. *Rossiiskaya gazeta*, October 7, 1992.

6. *Diplomaticheskii vestnik*, special edition, January 1993.

7. For the last 150 years, Russian society has been rocked by one form or another of the debates between "Westernizers," who feel that Russia must become fully integrated with the West in order to solve its

internal difficulties, and "Slavophiles," who see Russia as a civilization distinct from the West, with its own unique path of development.

8. E. M. Primakov, *Rossiya v mirovoi politike // God planety*, Moscow, 1998, p. 52.

9. *Vneshnyaya politika Rossii; mnenie exspertov*, Russian Independent Institute of Social and Nationalities Problems, Moscow, 2001, p. 10.

10. D. I. Mendeleev, *Granits poznaniyi predvidet' nevozmozhno*, Moscow, 1991, p. 101.

11. Such sentiments continue to be expressed today. At the World Council of Russian People in December 2001, Patriarch Alexiy II proclaimed, "Russia is destined to take part in solving problems facing the whole of mankind. . . . We feel ourselves as a bridge between the East and the West."

12. See Federal Law on State Policy of the Russian Federation with Respect to Compatriots Abroad, May 24, 1992.

13. *Bol'shoi entsiklopedicheskii slovar'*, Moscow, 1997, p. 954.

14. *Istoriya vneshnei politiki Rossii, konets XIX nachalo XX veka*, Moscow, 1997, p. 5.

15. Yu. Ya. Solov'ev, *Vospominaniya diplomata*, Moscow, 1959, p. 6.

16. G. Kennan, *Russian Foreign Policy: Essays in Historical Perspective*, Yale University Press, 1962, p. 595.

17. Ibid., p. 596.

18. *Diplomaticheskii vestnik*, 1992, no. 1, p. 13.

19. *Diplomaticheskii vestnik*, 1992, no. 2-3, p. 34.

20. Andrei Gromyko (1909–89) was one of the main participants in the creation of the postwar world order, as Soviet ambassador to the United States (1943–46), chief delegate to the United Nations (1946–48) and foreign minister (1957–85).

21. Gorchakov served as foreign minister and chancellor to Alexander II from 1867 to his resignation in 1882.

22. A. M. Kantsler, *Gorchakov, 200-letie so dnya rozhdeniya*, Moscow, 1998, pp. 321–322, 334.

23. Ibid., p. 334.

24. The Time of Troubles, which began after the death of Tsar Fedor in 1598, was marked by famine and civil strife within Russia and foreign intervention leading to the occupation of Moscow itself by Polish forces and the loss of territories in the northwest to Sweden. It ended with the election of Mikhail Romanov as tsar.

25. Prime Minister Petr Stolypin, during his tenure as head of the government (1906–11), sought to promote social stability through wide-ranging political and economic reforms, with the goal of creating a large body of middle-class peasant farmers.

26. S. D. Sazonov, *Vospominaniya*, Moscow, 1991, p. 343.

27. A. M. Kantsler, *Gorchakov, 200-letie so dnya rozhdeniya*, Moscow, 1998, p. 385.

28. The Decembrists were army officers who wanted to establish representative democracy in Russia, either under the aegis of a constitutional monarchy or as a republic. Upon the death of Emperor Alexander I in December 1825, they staged an abortive uprising in Palace Square in St. Petersburg, but the rebellion failed and many prominent aristocrats implicated in the revolt were exiled to Siberia.

29. A. M. Kantsler, *Gorchakov, 200-letie so dnya rozhdeniya*, Moscow, 1998, p. 388.

30. *Rossiiskaya diplomatiya v portretakh*, Moscow, 1992, p. 337.

31. S. D. Sazonov, *Vospominaniya*, Moscow, 1991, p. 353.

32. G. N. Mikhailovskii, *Zapiski: Iz istorii rossiiskogo vneshnepoliticheskogo vedomstva, 1914-1920*, Kn. 1, Moscow, 1993. pp. 78–79. The Black Hundreds were a protofascist movement in early modern Russia who organized attacks on liberal and socialist politicians and were determined to maintain the autocracy as a bulwark against modern and Western influences.

33. Consider, for example, the wide range of contacts enjoyed by Tsar Ivan IV ("the Terrible"), who corresponded with Queen Elizabeth I and welcomed English merchants to Russia, married a princess of the Nogai Tatars, and regularly interacted with sovereigns ranging from the Ottoman Sultan to the Holy Roman Emperor.

34. Ordin-Nashchokin's most significant endeavor was to conclude the agreement reached at Andruszowo in 1667, by which the Polish Commonwealth ceded the district of Smolensk and all Eastern Ukraine to Tsar Alexis; this treaty marked the definitive rise of Russia as a major power in Eastern Europe.

35. Among the most significant for the destiny of Russia were Peter's personal negotiations with King Frederick Augustus, ruler of Saxony and king of Poland; the meeting between these two monarchs in 1699 laid the foundation for the Great Northern War (1700–21) against Sweden.

36. This treaty gave Russian vessels access to the Black Sea, and also gave Russia the right to supervise the treatment of Eastern Christians within the Ottoman Empire and to make representations on their behalf. Most important, the treaty marks the extension of Russian influence into the Balkans and the Caucasus.

37. Quoted in: S. S. Ol'denburg, *Tsarstvovanie imperatora Nikolaya II*, Moscow, 1992. pp. 91–92.

38. As a leading expert in public and international law, Martens represented Russia at nearly every major international conference during his forty years of service with the Foreign Ministry. Martens's most important legacy is the so-called Martens clause, which has become an established part of international humanitarian law. It states that "civilians and combatants remain under the pro-

tection and authority of the principles of international law derived from established custom, from the principles of humanity and from the dictates of public conscience."

39. V. V. Pustogarov, *Fedor Fedorovich Martens, iurist, diplomat,* Moscow, 1999, p. 65.

40. *Vneshnyaya politika SSSR, Sbornik dokumentov, T. 1 (1917–1920 gg.),* Moscow, 1944, p. 26.

41. Chicherin had been a member of the Imperial foreign ministry but was forced to emigrate due to his Socialist Revolutionary sympathies following the 1905 Revolution. He returned to Russia in 1918 and succeeded Leon Trotsky as commissar of foreign affairs.

Chapter Two

1. *Rossiya i mir, Novyi kurs, Politicheskie rekomendatsii, osnovannye na mezhdunarodnom proekte "Okruzhayushchaya sreda rossiiskoi bezopasnosti,"* Moscow, 1999, p. 11.

2. *Ezhgodnik SIPRI, 1997,* Moscow, 1997, p. 35.

3. The term "rogue state" (and the less-inflammatory alternative, "states of concern") has been used by the United States to denote countries, usually developing ones, that are essentially hostile to the United States. The United States also accuses such states of developing weapons of mass destruction and sponsoring terrorism. Finally, the "rogue state" does not subscribe to what the United States regards as the norms of international behavior.

4. *Strategic Assessment,* Institute for National Strategic Studies, Washington, 1999, p. 14.

5. Ibid., p. 12.

6. Colloque de l'Institut de Relations Internationales et Strateguiques sur morale et relations internationales, May 16, 2000, Intervention d'ouverture du Ministre des Affaires Etrangeres, p. 4.

7. *Izvestiya,* May 15, 1999.

8. Article 52.1 of the UN Charter declares, "Nothing in the present Charter precludes the existence of regional arrangements or agencies for dealing with such matters relating to the maintenance of international peace and security as are appropriate for regional action provided that such arrangements or agencies and their activities are consistent with the Purposes and Principles of the United Nations." The Charter goes on to say, in Article 53.1, "The Security Council shall, where appropriate, utilize such regional arrangements or agencies for enforcement action under its authority. But no enforcement action shall be taken under regional arrangements or by regional agencies without the authorization of the Security Council, with the exception of measures against any enemy state, as

defined in paragraph 2 of this Article, provided for pursuant to Article 107 or in regional arrangements directed against renewal of aggressive policy on the part of any such state, until such time as the Organization may, on request of the Governments concerned, be charged with the responsibility for preventing further aggression by such a state."

9. Karl-Heinz Kamp, "L'OTAN après le Kosovo, ange de paix ou gendarme du monde?" *Politique Etrangere*, no. 2, 1999, p. 255.

10. Adopted on June 10, 1999, this resolution "authorizes the Secretary-General, with the assistance of relevant international organizations, to establish an international civil presence in Kosovo in order to provide an interim administration for Kosovo under which the people of Kosovo can enjoy substantial autonomy within the Federal Republic of Yugoslavia," and "demands that the KLA and other armed Kosovo Albanian groups end immediately all offensive actions and comply with the requirements for demilitarization as laid down by the head of the international security presence in consultation with the Special Representative of the Secretary-General."

11. Samuel P. Huntington, "The Lonely Superpower," *Foreign Affairs*, March–April 1999, p. 37.

12. *Strategiya dlya Rossii: povestka dnya dlya Prezidenta—2000 (doklad Soveta po vneshnei i oboronnoi politike)*, Moscow, 2000, p. 91.

13. Jacques Chirac, "La France dans un Monde Multipolair," *Politique Etrangere*, no. 4, 1999, p. 85.

14. *Final Document of the XIII Ministerial Conference of the Non-Aligned Countries*, Cartageña, April 8–9, 2000, para. 263; *Declaration of the South Summit*, Havana, April 10–14, 2000, para 54.

15. *Final Document of the XIII Ministerial Conference of the Non-Aligned Countries*, Cartageña, April 8–9, 2000, para. 11.

16. International Monetary Fund, *World Economic Outlook*, May 1997, p. 45.

17. Paul Arnaud de Foiard, "Liberalisme et humanisme," *Défense Nationale*, no. 11, 1999, pp. 10–11.

18. Tenth United Nations Congress on the Prevention of Crime and the Treatment of Offenders, DPI/2088/F-003219, United Nations, p. 1.

19. See *Sbornik deistvuyushchikh dogovorov, soglashenii i konventsii, zaklyuchennykh SSSR s inostrannymi gosudarstvami, Vyp. 28*, Moscow, 1974, pp. 31–35.

20. See G. A. Trofimenko and P. T. Podlesnyi, eds, *Sovetsko-amerikanskie otnosheniya v sovremennom mire*, Moscow, 1997, ch. 4; A. Dobrynin, *Sugubo doveritel'no, Posol v Vashingtone pri shesti prezidentakh SShA (1962–1986)*, Moscow, 1996; H. Kissinger, *Diplomatiya*, Moscow, 1997, ch. 29.

21. On June 13, 1991, the USSR declared that the START I treaty would be "effective and viable only under conditions of compliance" with the 1972 ABM Treaty.

22. This is provided for in the Federal Law on Ratification of the Treaty between the Russian Federation and the United States of America on Further Reduction and Limitation of Strategic Offensive Arms, adopted in April 2000. Article 2(b) authorizes the government of the Russian Federation to withdraw from the treaty in the event of U.S. withdrawal from or infringement of the ABM Treaty.

23. This refers to the decision by the United States not to completely destroy MX Peacekeeper missiles, as provided for by the treaty, but to destroy only the upper stage of the missile, leaving the first stage intact. The Russian foreign ministry publicly protested U.S. actions on January 4, 2001.

24. For example, the Theater High-Altitude Area Defense (THAAD) system and the Navy Theater-Wide Ballistic Missile Defense program on the U.S. side, and the S-300V system on the Russian side.

25. The MTCR was established in April, 1987. It presently includes thirty-three member-states: NATO and the EU, as well as Australia, Argentina, Brazil, New Zealand, Ukraine, Switzerland, South Africa, South Korea, Japan, and the Russian Federation (which has been a full member since 1995).

26. "We the Peoples: The Role of the United Nations in the 21st Century," Report by UN Secretary-General Kofi Annan, A/54/2000, presented to the General Assembly, April 3, 2000, para. 362.

27. "Report of the Secretary-General on the Work of the Organization," Official Notes of the General Assembly, 50th Session, addendum no.1 (A/50/1), paras. 2–3.

28. In addition to appealing for continued adherence to the ABM Treaty, the resolution also called for concerted efforts to preserve the UN's role as the cornerstone of global strategic stability, world peace, and strategic nuclear arms reductions. It also urged all UN member-states to support efforts to stem the proliferation of weapons of mass destruction and their means of delivery.

29. *Final Document of the XIII Ministerial Conference of the Non-Aligned Countries,* Cartageña, April 8–9, 2000, paras. 29–30.

30. United Nations document E/CN.4/1998/53, February 11, 1998, p. 2.

31. World Refugee Survey, 1998, p. 3.

32. Charter of the United Nations, ch. VI, arts. 33–38; ch. VII, arts. 39–51.

Chapter Three

1. Belarus, Russia, and Ukraine signed the initial agreement creating the CIS on December 8, 1991. Subsequently, at the summit held in Alma-Ata on December 21, 1991, the protocol to this agreeement was signed by Armenia, Azerbaijan, Belarus, Kazakhstan, Kyrgyzstan, Moldova, the Russian Federation, Tajikistan, Turkmenistan, Ukraine, and Uzbekistan. Georgia joined the CIS on December 9, 1993.

2. The CIS-CHS and CIS-CHG have begun to recognize the need to close the gap between rhetoric and reality. At the November 30–December 1, 2000, meeting in Minsk, an inventory authorized by the CIS-CHS at the CIS summit of April 2, 1999, reported that forty-one treaties concluded within the CIS and 122 decisions of the CIS-CHS were no longer valid.

3. "Strategicheskii kurs Rossii s gosudarstvami-uchastniki Sodruzhestva Nezavisimykh Gosudarstv," *Diplomaticheskii vestnik*, no. 10, 1995.

4. "Dogovor o sozdanii Soyuznogo gosudarstva Rossii i Belorussii," *Rossiiskaya gazeta*, January 29, 2000.

5. "Dogovor mezhdu Respublikoi Belorussiya, Respublikoi Kazakhstan, Kirgizskoi Respublikoi, i Rossiiskoi Federatsiei ob uglublenii integratsii v ekonomicheskoi i gumanitarnoi oblastyakh, Moskva, 29 marta, 1996 g.," in *Vneshnyaya politika i bezopasnost' sovremennoi Rossii. Khrestomatiya, Tom 2*, Moscow, 1999, pp. 353–58.

6. The treaty was first ratified in 1994. When it expired in 1999, Azerbaijan, Georgia, and Uzbekistan declined to renew their participation. At present, the parties to the treaty are Armenia, Belarus, Kazakhstan, Kyrgyzstan, Russia, and Tajikistan.

7. At the Ninth Meeting of the Ministerial Council of the OSCE, held December 3–4, 2001, in Bucharest, it was noted: "We welcome the fulfillment by the Russian Federation, ahead of the agreed time, of the commitments undertaken at the OSCE Istanbul Summit in 1999 on withdrawal and disposal of the CFE Treaty-Limited Equipment located in the Transdniestrian region of the Republic of Moldova by the end of 2001. We commend the Russian Federation on its accomplishment, as well as the other parties for their contribution to this achievement. We believe this should serve as a model for constructive and fruitful co-operation in dealing with other issues."

8. Kasymzhomart Tokaev, *Vneshnyaya politika Kazakhstana v usloviyakh globalizatsii*, Almaty, 2000, p. 224.

9. See *Ot Khelsinki do Budapeshta. Istoriya SBSE/OBSE v dokumentakh, 1973-1994, Tom 3*, Moscow, 1997, pp. 464–512.

10. Article 12 of the Charter for European Security reads: "We pledge ourselves, through the Platform for Co-operative Security, which is hereby adopted as an essential element of this Charter, to further strengthen and develop cooperation with competent organizations on the basis of equality and in a spirit of partnership. The principles of the Platform for Co-operative Security, as set out in the operational document attached to this Charter, apply to any organization or institution whose members individually and collectively decide to adhere to them. They apply across all dimensions of security; politico-military, human, and economic. Through this Platform we seek to develop and maintain political and operational coherence, on the basis of shared values, among all the various bodies dealing with security, both in responding to specific crises and in formulating responses to new risks and challenges."

11. The Bucharest meeting led to the adoption of an Action Plan designed to promote "comprehensive OSCE action to be taken by participating States and the Organization as a whole to combat terrorism, fully respecting international law, including the international law of human rights and other relevant norms of international law. The Action Plan seeks to expand existing activities that contribute to combating terrorism, facilitate interaction between States and, where appropriate, identify new instruments for action. The Action Plan, which recognizes that the fight against terrorism requires sustained efforts, will identify activities to be implemented immediately as well as over the medium and long term."

12. See "Ustav Soveta Evropy," *Diplomaticheskii vestnik,* no. 4, 1996, pp. 30–50; A. H. Robertson, *The Council of Europe: Its Structure, Functions and Achievements,* London, 1956.

13. See *Konventsii Soveta Evropy i Rossiiskaya Federatsiya, Sbornik dokumentov,* Moscow, 2000; S. A. Glotov, *Rossiya i Sovet Evropy: politiko-pravovye problemy vzaimodeistviya,* Krasnodar, 1998.

14. See *Konventsii Soveta Evropy i Rossiiskaya Federatsiya, Sbornik dokumentov,* Moscow, 2000; *Pravo Soveta Evropy i Rossiya, Sbornik dokumentov i materialov, Izd. 2-e, dop,* Krasnodar, 1996; *Rossiya v Sovete Evropy,* Moscow, 1999.

15. See the text of "Politicheskaya Deklaratsiya," *Diplomaticheskii vestnik,* no. 6, 1999, pp. 36–37.

16. See Resolution of the Government of the Russian Federation, no. 33, December 4, 2000; "Ob odobrenii predlozheniya o podmisanii Evropeiskoi sotsial'noi khartii," *Sobranie zakonodatel'stva Rossiiskoi Federatsii,* no. 6, 2000, p. 1732.

17. See "Soglashenie o partnerstve i sotrudnichestve meshdu Rossiiskoi Federatsiei i Evropeiskim soyuzom. Iyun' 1994," in *Dokumenty, kasayushchiesya vzaimootnoshenii mezhdu Evropeiskim soyuzom i Rossiei,* Moscow, 1994, pp. 84–210.

18. The joint declaration commits both the EU and the Russian Federation to "institute specific consultations on security and defense matters at the appropriate level and in the appropriate format; develop strategic dialogue on matters, particularly in regard to security, which have implications for the Russian Federation and the European Union; extend the scope of regular consultations at expert level on the issues of disarmament, arms control and non-proliferation; promote cooperation in operational crisis management."

19. Texts of these plans can be found in *Traktaty o vechnom mire,* Moscow, 1963.

20. "Osnovopolagayushchii akt o vzaimnykh otnosheniyakh, sotrudnichestve, i bezopasnosti mezhdu Organizatsiei Severoatlanticheskogo dogovora i Rossiiskoi Federatsiei," *Diplomaticheskii vestnik,* no. 6, 1997 pp. 4–9.

21. At Feira, the European Council endorsed the Action Plan for the Northern Dimension, inviting the Commission to draft follow-up proposals that would address, among other things, environmental and nuclear safety and the status of Kaliningrad.

22. Some of these proposals were incorporated into the "Joint Statement on Cooperation on Strategic Stability," adopted in Okinawa on July 21, 2000.

23. The joint statement issued on June 5, 2000, states that both presidents "agree that the international community faces a dangerous and growing threat of proliferation of weapons of mass destruction and their means of delivery, including missiles and missile technologies, and stress their desire to reverse that process, including through existing and possible new international legal mechanisms. They agree that this new threat represents a potentially significant change in the strategic situation and international security environment. They agree that this emerging threat to security should be addressed and resolved through mutual cooperation and mutual respect of each other's security interests."

24. The Wassenaar Arrangement on Export Controls for Conventional Arms and Dual-Use Goods and Technologies was established in 1995 in order to contribute to regional and international security and stability by promoting transparency and greater responsibility in transfers of conventional arms and dual-use goods and technologies, thus preventing destabilizing accumulations. Participating states will seek, through their national policies, to ensure that transfers of these items do not contribute to the development or enhancement of military capabilities which undermine these goals and are not diverted to support such capabilities. The participating states include Argentina, Australia, Austria, Belgium, Bulgaria, Canada, the Czech Republic, Denmark, Finland, France, Germany, Greece, Hungary, Ireland, Italy, Japan, Luxembourg, the Netherlands, New Zealand, Norway, Poland, Portugal, the Republic of Korea, Romania, the Russian Federation, Slovakia, Spain, Sweden, Switzerland, Turkey, Ukraine, the United Kingdom, and the United States.

25. Charter for European Security, Istanbul, November 18, 1999.

26. Many of the goals outlined above were included in the joint declaration. In part, the statement reads: "We support the building of a European-Atlantic community whole, free, and at peace, excluding no one, and respecting the independence, sovereignty and territorial integrity of all nations. To this end, the United States and Russia will work, together with NATO and other NATO members, to improve, strengthen, and enhance the relationship between NATO and Russia, with a view to developing new, effective mechanisms for consultation, cooperation, joint decision, and coordinated/joint action. We believe that these mechanisms should reflect the fact that the members of NATO and Russia are increasingly allied against terrorism, regional instability and other contemporary threats, and that the NATO-Russia relationship should therefore evolve

accordingly. We will also work to strengthen our cooperation in OSCE as a broadly representative, inclusive organization for conducting consultations, taking decisions, and working together in the region. We recognize a market economy, the freedom of economic choice and an open democratic society as the most effective means to provide for the welfare of our citizens. The United States and Russia will cooperate, including through the support of direct contacts between the business communities of our countries, to advance U.S.-Russian economic, trade, and investment relations. The achievement of these goals requires the removal of legislative and administrative barriers, a transparent, predictable investment climate, the rule of law, and market-based economic reforms."

27. A. M. Kantsler, *Gorchakov: 200 letie so dnya rozhdeniya*, Moscow, 1998. pp. 271–72.

28. "Rossiisko-kitaiskaya sovmestnaya deklaratsiya o mnogopolyarnom mire i formirovanii novogo mezhdunarodnogo poryadka," Moscow, April 23, 1997, in *Vneshnyaya politika i bezopasnost' sovremennoi Rossii, Khrestomatiya, Tom 2*, pp. 478–80.

29. The treaty, signed July 16, 2001, contains a number of key provisions, including (1) a commitment to develop a strategic, cooperative partnership; (2) absolute support for the national unity and territorial integrity of the other party; (3) a pledge that neither side will join any alliance that harms the other's sovereignty, security, or territorial integrity; and (4) a commitment to enhance the central role of the United Nations in international affairs.

30. The strategic partnership agreement between India and Russia was characterized by Prime Minister Vajpayee as a "firm and long-term commitment to work in close cooperation as partners on all issues, including political, international, and economic [ones]." Statement of the prime minister, October 3, 2000.

31. The Moscow Declaration states that shared democratic values between Russia and Japan serve as the basis for partnership and cooperation. Both parties agreed to resume efforts to find a permanent and lasting solution to the problems of the Kuril islands. Russia also expressed support for Japan's bid to acquire a permanent seat on the UN Security Council.

32. V. V. Putin, "Rossiya: novye vostochnye perspektivy," *Nezavisimaya gazeta*, November 14, 2000.

33. To facilitate its goals, which include combating terrorism, extremism, and smuggling, the Shanghai Cooperation Organization (SCO) plans to organize an annual meeting of the heads of states and facilitate contacts between the various agencies of the member-states. Moreover, the SCO is examining the creation of expert groups, both temporary and permanent, to prepare proposals to enhance the cooperative efforts of its members.

34. In 2000, it was reported that three-quarters of all deliveries from Russian civil aircraft manufacturers to customers during the last year went to Egypt.

35. The qualitative growth in ties between Latin America and Russia was convincingly demonstrated following the first Russia–Latin America business forum, which was held in Moscow, June 25–29, 2001. The forum provided an opportunity for participants to examine ways to streamline trade, economic, and scientific links between Russia and Latin America and the Caribbean.

36. The treaty, signed on February 14, 1967, was created in response to UN General Assembly resolution 808 (IX), which calls for a coordinated program of disarmament leading to "the total prohibition of the use and manufacture of nuclear weapons and weapons of mass destruction of every type."

37. The joint statement issued by the presidents of Cuba and Russia on December 14, 2000, reiterated that both nations intend to develop bilateral cooperation and declared the need for all states to observe the provisions of the UN Charter.

Chapter Four

1. Data obtained from customs statistics detailing the foreign trade of the Russian Federation.

2. Many of these matters are covered under title III of the agreement, which entered into force on December 1, 1997.

3. A. Shishaev, "Sredstva torgovoi zashchity: antidempingovye mery (opyt ES)," *Yuridicheskii mir*, nos. 9–10, 1998, pp. 48–57.

4. This strategy is designed to serve as the basis for an "active dialogue" and constructive proposals for shaping relations between Russia, the European Union, and the EU's member-states.

5. Text in *Rossiiskaya gazeta*, January 16, 1999. This legislation helped to clear up many ambiguities that had existed for much of the 1990s. It spelled out the rights of local and regional bodies to conduct direct negotiations with foreign entities (article 2); created a "reconciliation process" by which draft agreements concluded by the regions are subject to review by the Foreign Ministry (article 4); clarified the status of formal offices opened by regions and localities abroad (article10); and set up a mechanism for dispute resolution between the federal center and the regions (article 12).

6. In full, article 73 reads: "The Parties shall strengthen cooperation between them on regional development and land-use planning. They shall encourage exchange of information by national, regional and local authorities on regional and land-use planning policy and on methods of formulation of regional policies with special emphasis on the development of disadvantaged areas. They shall also encourage direct contacts between the respective regions and public organizations responsible for regional development planning with the aim, inter alia, to exchange methods and ways of fostering regional development."

7. 1980 European Outline Convention on Transfrontier Cooperation between Territorial Communities or Authorities, Madrid, May 21, 1980. Published in *Konventsiya Soveta Evropy i Rossiiskaya Federatsiya, Sbornik dokumentov*, Moscow: Yuridicheskaya literatura, 2000, pp. 298–370.

8. The term "near abroad" is used by many Russians to refer to the other republics of the former Soviet Union; it conveys the sense that these areas, while not juridically part of the Russian state (and thus "beyond the border"), do share elements of a common historical experience, and in addition may contain large numbers of ethnic Russians. Thus, they are not as "foreign" to Russia as other areas of the world.

9. Griboedov, for example, is renowned both for his skill as a diplomat and as the author of the play "Gore ot Uma" ("Woe from wit"). He was killed when a mob attacked the Russian embassy in Teheran.

INDEX

Cold war, 24, 93. *See also* Soviet foreign policy
Collective Security Treaty (CIS), 88
College of Foreign Affairs, 31
Colombia, 136, 137
Commonwealth of Independent States (CIS): Central Asia security, 86–87; Collective Security Treaty, 88; cultural exchange with Russia, 156; economic ties with Russia, 144; establishment of, 82; goals of, 82, 83, 88; market reforms, 82–83, 144; nuclear disarmament supported, 88; peacekeeping by Russia, 89; Russia's relationship with, 35, 81–92, 144, 153; Shanghai Cooperation Organization membership, 128; Strategic Course of Russia with Member States of, 84; terrorism opposed, 88; third-party states acting in, 87; trade with Russia, 86, 92; treaties with Russia, 85; UN peacekeeping, 89. *See also specific member states*
Comprehensive Test Ban Treaty (CTBT), 60, 67, 68, 125
Concept for Peace in the Twenty-First Century, 45
Conference on Disarmament, 68
Congress of Vienna, 36
Continuity in Russian foreign policy, 9, 161; anti-isolationism, 30, 34; definition of, 17; and diplomacy, 36–37; enlightened patriotism, 29; and national security, 30; negative historical implications, 34–35; scientific approach, 25–26; of Soviet goals, 19–25; stability of relations and, 18, 33; of Tsarist goals, 19, 28–29, 30–33
Convention against Transnational Organized Crime, 75
Convention on Chemical Weapons, 25

Convention on Financial Terrorism, 69, 75
Convention on Laws and Customs of War on Land, 32
Convention on the Elimination of all Forms of Discrimination against Women, 70
Convention on the Rights of the Child, 70
Conventional Forces in Europe (CFE) Treaty, 91
Coordinating Committee on Multilateral Export Controls (COCOM), 114
Council of Baltic States (CBSS), 108, 109, 152
Council of Europe, 99, 100–02
Crime. *See* Organized crime
CTBT. *See* Comprehensive Test Ban Treaty
Cuba, 137, 138
Cultural diversity, 55, 102
Cultural foreign policy, 154–59; and CIS relations, 156; Leadership Council for Russian Science, Education, and Culture, 155; Pushkin bicentennial, 157; UNESCO, 157–58

Declaration on Strategic Partnership between Russia and India (*2000*), 123
Défense Nationale, 54
Democratization: and global security, 41–42; of Russian society and foreign policy, 16–17
Digital divide, 53
Diplomacy: and culture in foreign relations, 154–58; definition, 36; negotiation required, 159; role in foreign relations, 36–37; as science, 158–59, 163

UNESCO, 157–58
Union Treaty between Belarus and
    Russia, 85
Unipolar world of U.S. foreign policy,
    43–45; global hegemony pursued by,
    46, 118
United Nations (UN): charter viola-
    tions, 23–24, 44, 45, 51, 69, 98; and
    CIS peacekeeping, 89; disarmament
    support, 64–65, 74; economic initia-
    tives, 76; equitable approach, 73;
    importance, 72; international secu-
    rity actions, 69; Millennium
    Assembly, 68; NATO actions violat-
    ing principles of, 44, 51; Peace
    Support Operations, 73, 89; reforms,
    77, 114; refugees and internally dis-
    placed persons, 76; role in multipo-
    lar world system, 48, 49–50, 70, 71,
    77–79; and Russian Federation, 22,
    71–79; sanctions as strategy, 74–75,
    132; and Yugoslavia situation, 44, 74.
    See also UN Security Council; and
    conventions by name
U.S. foreign policy: sanctions, 50; global
    hegemony pursued, 46, 118; mental-
ity of cold war victor, 43, 111–12;
    missile defense system, 60; and
    NATO expansion, 12; unilateral
    approach, 43–45, 50. See also Russia-
    U.S. relationship
U.S. Friendship Act, 115–16
USSR. See Former Soviet republics;
    Soviet foreign policy
Uzbekistan, 128. See also
    Commonwealth of Independent
    States

Védrine, Hubert, 43, 110
Viskovaty, Ivan Mikhailovich, 30

Waasenaar Arrangement, 114
Western vs. Eastern influence in Russian
    foreign policy, 33–34
Women, 70
World Bank, 76
World Trade Organization (WTO),
    143–44, 148

Yeltsin, Boris, 11, 84
Yugoslavia, 43, 44, 50, 74, 106. See also
    NATO